THE AUTOBIOGRAPHY OF
CALVIN COOLIDGE

THE AUTOBIOGRAPHY OF
CALVIN COOLIDGE

AUTHORIZED, EXPANDED, AND
ANNOTATED EDITION

Edited with an introduction by
AMITY SHLAES AND
MATTHEW DENHART

**ISI
BOOKS**

Wilmington, DE

This book was made possible through the generous support of Philip Gasiewicz, the JM Foundation, Michael and Andrea Leven, Robert L. Luddy, Jacqueline G. Mock, Peter Morse, Thomas J. Posatko, Tanner Industries, and other supporters.

Library of Congress Control Number: 2020947192

ISBN: 978-1-61017-163-2

Published in the United States by:

ISI Books
Intercollegiate Studies Institute
3901 Centerville Road
Wilmington, Delaware 19807-1938
www.isibooks.org

Manufactured in the United States of America

CONTENTS

HE LIVED BY EXAMPLE

BY AMITY SHLAES AND
MATTHEW DENHART

P residents loom over America, and so must their monuments. That was the conviction of the sculptor Gutzon
Borglum as he laid his dynamite at Mount Rushmore
in the summer of 1927. At Rushmore, Borglum would blast and
hack at the mountain until it yielded up the visages of George
Washington, Thomas Jefferson, Abraham Lincoln, and Theodore Roosevelt—each face sixty feet tall. The president at the
time, Calvin Coolidge, happened to be in South Dakota and
rode up the mountain on a horse named Mistletoe to preside
at the groundbreaking of Borglum's gargantuan project. The
sculptor, elated, and doubtless aiming to please the president,
told the crowd that one day a mega-bust of Coolidge could join
those of his four predecessors in the granite. "This colossus is
our mark," Borglum later said, the mark of a great civilization
built by great men.

But Coolidge wanted no colossus. The film footage from
the groundbreaking ceremony shows the thirtieth president
duly delivering remarks—and then turning off from the scene,

rather too quickly. The reporters present guessed that the fifty-five-year-old chief executive was worried about another matter. Coolidge had come to the presidency in 1923 upon the death of Warren Harding. Americans had given him a resounding victory when he ran for office on his own in 1924. Polls suggested Coolidge remained overwhelmingly popular leading up to 1928. Now, therefore, his fellow politicians and his party were pressuring Coolidge to announce he would run again.

A few days before his ride up Rushmore, Coolidge had sought to end the election discussion. The president asked his deputy to type up and hand out a statement to the reporters in attendance at the Summer White House, a temporary office in the high school at Rapid City. The statement was a single line: "I do not choose to run for President in nineteen twenty eight."

The statement had not halted the pressure. The pressmen could not believe what they read and commenced pestering Coolidge, following him everywhere, even between the pines up to Rushmore. What leader turns his back on a guaranteed reelection? Surely, Coolidge did not mean what he wrote. Perhaps the president would reverse his position in a few days—a call from Republican leadership to South Dakota might change his mind. Or perhaps, the pressmen speculated, Coolidge suffered from some unannounced and grave malady—poor health could be the reason for Coolidge's unexpected retreat.

The reason for Coolidge's decision not to run was indeed health—not the president's health but the health of our democracy. In fact, Coolidge's decision to walk away from Rushmore and his decision to walk away from the presidency were linked. They came out of his own conviction, one different from the sculptor's. In the Coolidge conviction, the power of America lay not in great men but in great institutions, institutions in turn built on their own bedrock, the rock of principle. Because of those institutions, American citizens enjoyed rights and freedoms, he later wrote, that made them the "peer of kings." Such people were best governed by principles, not potentates. The continued success of the nation depended on the popular commitment to those principles and institutions, not to men. "The progress of America has been due to the spirit of the people," Coolidge said at Rushmore. Hero worship might make Americans forget that laws mattered more than men. Like Washington, who doubtless would have bridled at the sight of himself on the skyline, Coolidge believed presidents were there to preside, not rule. Modesty in a president was wisest.

Coolidge would make the case for the primacy of such principles in the autobiography in your hands. "It is a great advantage to a President, and a major source of safety to the country," Coolidge wrote, "for him to know that he is not a great man." The longer a president stayed in office, the closer he moved toward tyranny. Another safeguard, therefore, was to rotate the office holder. "The chances of having wise and faithful public service are increased by a change in the Presidential office after a moderate length of time," Coolidge elaborated. In South Dakota and after, Coolidge stuck to his decision about the presidency. No amount of berating or cajoling changed his mind. Following the March 1929 inauguration of Herbert Hoover, he and Mrs. Coolidge rode the train back to New England, returning to their modest duplex on Massasoit Street in Northampton, Massachusetts.

The South Dakota summer was not the final time Coolidge rejected the grandiose. In 1931 the former president traveled to Marion, Ohio, to dedicate another vast monument, a marble-pillared shrine to his predecessor, Warren Harding. His own grave, Coolidge determined, would be different. When he passed away, in January 1933, the Coolidge family, respecting his wishes, laid the president to rest in the Coolidge row in the modest cemetery at his birthplace, Plymouth Notch, Vermont. The tallest stone in the row is that of Coolidge's grandfather, Calvin Galusha Coolidge. Coolidge's own gravestone stands no higher than that of his wife, Grace. The only sign that the grave is a former president's is the presidential seal chiseled into the granite.

COOLIDGE'S STUDIED MODESTY SEEMS strange in our day. Perhaps that is one reason Coolidge gets scant space in our history books. Some authors take Coolidge's restraint for weakness and make a stereotype of him: Silent Cal, a Puritan throwback, an arch-conservative, a man with no skill in newer media. Others treat the president from New England as a kind of seat warmer between giants such as Theodore Roosevelt and his cousin Franklin. These authors dismiss Coolidge as an accident, emphasizing that only the death of Harding put him in office in the first place. Still others blame Coolidge for causing the Great Depression of the 1930s, though the evidence for this allegation is missing. As often as anything else, Coolidge is simply forgotten.

But Coolidge should not be forgotten. For in many respects Coolidge confounds stereotype. As governor, for example, the "arch-conservative" Coolidge backed a number of progressive measures and counseled against legislating as an ideologue: "Don't hesitate to be as revolutionary as science. Don't hesitate to be as reactionary as the multiplication table." Perhaps because he knew what it was like to live in Plymouth, to which the railroad had not chosen to come, this old-fashioned president exhibited a modern passion for technology and networks. Because so few radio recordings exist, few today know that Coolidge starred in what is today known as Franklin Roosevelt's medium, radio. Coolidge's nasal voice cut through the airwaves like wire, it was said. As president, "Silent Cal" gave hundreds of press conferences and established "a record for speechmaking in the last two decades," the *New York Times* reported in February 1929. Coolidge devoted much time to his speeches and only rarely allowed others to write them. You will find several of his most important speeches in the appendix to this edition of his autobiography.

The extent to which commentators distort Coolidge is evident in the way they cite one of his more famous lines: "The chief business of the American people is business." Coolidge's detractors seize on this statement—which they often misquote as "the business of America is business"—to portray the president as a tool of big business, concerned with nothing but material success. They fail to mention that in the same speech, delivered in 1925, Coolidge said, "The chief ideal of the American people is idealism." He added that Americans are not "absorbed by material motives," that "there are many other things that we want very much more." In another speech, Coolidge acknowledged that "we live in an age of science and of abounding accumulation of material things" but also said that "the things of the spirit come first."

Coolidge's restraint did not come out of weakness. The restraint reflected discipline, which is why those who like Coolidge call him the Great Refrainer. Today Americans expect presidents to charge ahead, waving multipoint plans to address the issues confronting their people. Coolidge knew what the Framers knew: that there exist many problems the government cannot solve, and there is much an executive should not attempt. The principles Coolidge recognized as key—civility, bipartisanship, federalism, government thrift, and respect for enterprise and religious faith—are ones many Americans long to see revived. These principles come straight from the Founders and served as the basis for our civilization long before that.

"Men do not make laws," Coolidge once told the Massachusetts senate. "They do but discover them."

As important, however, is the fashion in which Coolidge advanced his principles. He did not merely talk them up, as a radio host might. Rather, he lived by example.

This book, composed as Coolidge was leaving Washington, demonstrates dramatically the power of such a life. Watching his father preside at the Plymouth Notch town meetings, the quiet red-haired boy saw that more was achieved when citizens worked together. He made a habit of practicing civility. Coolidge did not attend law school—his family found the tuition too pricey. Coolidge "read law," preparing for the Massachusetts bar by clerking at the Northampton firm of Hammond and Field. As he carried his books between the office and Forbes Library, where he studied cases and pored over old law texts, Coolidge developed a great respect for America's common-law tradition and the value of gradual change. By nature more solicitor than barrister, the young attorney chose to settle and save his clients money rather than rage, litigate, and bill.

Coolidge entered political life in a dramatic era, when, as today, flamboyant postures struck by politicians drew votes. Coolidge preferred to work his way up from within—within his party, that is. That party was the progressive party of the era, the Republican Party. Starting in city government in Northampton, the young attorney moved step by step from state representative on to mayor of Northampton, state senator, president of the senate, lieutenant governor, and, eventually, governor of the Bay State. Whether in work or in politics, Coolidge eschewed marketing himself for a promotion. Instead, as he told his friend Dwight Morrow, he determined to do such a good job that others—employers, voters—would give him that promotion. And they did.

New laws might be necessary, Coolidge saw as legislator, but older laws needed a chance: "Give administration a chance to catch up with legislation," he counseled in 1914, in his inaugural speech as president of the Massachusetts state senate. Sometimes, Coolidge said, the problem was simply too many laws: "It is much more important to kill bad bills than to pass good ones," he wrote to his father once.

An event in September 1919, when Coolidge was serving as Massachusetts governor, tested Coolidge's willingness to stand on principle. The immigrant vote had propelled him to office. Irish Americans had come out especially strong for Coolidge, and the Republican Party counted on their votes in that fall's election. When the Boston police, largely Irish Americans, walked out on strike, they doubtless expected some lenience from the governor. With the police off the job, rioting ensued, and the police approached Coolidge about negotiating their return. But the governor noted that the police contract permitted no such strike. Just because the police didn't like conditions in Boston did not mean they could strike. Coolidge backed up the police commissioner in the firing of the strikers, knowing full well the move might lose him the election that was to come just months later. "There is no right to strike against the public safety," Coolidge wrote in a terse telegram to labor leader Samuel Gompers, "by anybody, anywhere, any time."

The national mood that Coolidge confronted when he arrived in Washington as vice president in 1921 bore striking similarities to our own. Then, as now, the federal household reeled under the burden of an unpredicted debt, in that case generated by World War I. Then, as now, the expansion of what we would call entitlements seemed inevitable: two powerful groups, farmers—then far more numerous—and veterans, sought greater and more systematic spending in their behalf.

Then, as now, Americans divided, with progressives demanding radical laws and radical new institutions. Then, as now, racial tensions ran high, and indeed even higher than today: in the 1920s the Ku Klux Klan was lynching black Americans. Then, as now, the federal government seemed bound to take over work that heretofore had belonged to the states or towns.

From the moment he learned he would be president— in the first hours of August 3, 1923—Coolidge determined to bring America back to a commonsense course, not by lecturing the country but, again, by exemplifying key principles. His father was a notary public and swore Coolidge in by lamplight: a symbol of the authority of the local even in the gravest matters of our republic. Arriving in Washington, Coolidge promised to bring divided Americans together, and he worked with his political opponents to do so. America had prevailed in World War I, but its status as new world power was far from assured. That assurance would come only if the federal household were in better shape than that of Britain. Coolidge therefore committed to reducing the federal debt, telling Americans: "I am for economy. After that I am for more economy." Finally, the new president recognized the power of commerce. He committed to fostering conditions that would allow the private sector to grow, including cutting burdensome income taxes. Growth, Coolidge reasoned, would not only fill federal coffers but also improve the quality of life for all citizens, including the disadvantaged. Idealism and economic growth did not clash, as we are told today. Rather, they worked together.

As president, Coolidge bent his energies to seeing through laws that would advance his principles. He signed legislation that made all Native Americans citizens for the first time. Coolidge's support for African Americans was strong and explicit. When a correspondent wrote to ask him whether it was appropriate for a black American to run for Congress, Coolidge issued and published a scalding response, writing that he was "amazed" that anyone would doubt black Americans' right to participate to the fullest extent in politics. Coolidge believed the nation owed African Americans an opportunity to advance through education. Normally parsimonious, he supported an appropriation to benefit the medical school at Howard University, a federally chartered historically black institution in Washington, D.C. He also spoke at Howard's commencement.

Coolidge took the opportunity of the 150th anniversary of the Declaration of Independence to give a speech underscoring the rights of all Americans. The Declaration and the Constitution assured those rights; no storm of legislative activity could add to the commitment already made. "If all men are created equal, that is final," he said in that speech. "If they are endowed with inalienable rights, that is final. If governments derive their just power from the consent of the governed, that is final." He concluded, "No advance, no progress can be made beyond these propositions." Coolidge backed restriction in immigration not out of xenophobia but because he believed that America needed to settle down after the ruction and tragedy of World War I. He saw value in an America that itself lived by example. As many the world over attest, the symbol of the American "city on a hill" can have more power to reduce tyranny overseas than the arrival of gunboats or missiles. At Omaha, speaking to the American Legion in 1925, Coolidge told a vast crowd that whether Americans had come over on the *Mayflower* three centuries ago or in the steerage of an immigrant ship three years ago, "we are all now in the same boat."

Delegation was another principle Coolidge prized, and he followed the lead of his Treasury secretary, Andrew Mellon, in cutting taxes, bringing the key top marginal income tax rate down to 25 percent. The tax reductions inspired business, and in fact more money flowed into federal coffers than simple arithmetic had predicted. But Coolidge, warier than Mellon of what we could call a supply-side experiment, believed that federal budget cuts must accompany tax cuts. Coolidge cut the federal budget rather than contenting himself with reducing its increase.

To signal his commitment to government thrift, Coolidge demonstrated thrift in his private life. The White House entertainment spending seemed to him extravagant—it was time to serve fewer hams, he informed an astounded housekeeper. Likening his budget cutting to his father's work in Vermont, he called the tiny cuts he made here and there "cheese paring." Even the White House pets did not escape the Coolidge thrift campaign. Other first families give their pets lovable names— Barney, the Bush dog; Socks, the Clinton cat. Not the Coolidges: when the president received twin lion cubs as a gift, Coolidge pointedly named the pair "Tax Reduction" and "Budget Bureau."

When the president encountered a bill that increased federal spending, he generally vetoed it—even with the knowledge that Congress might override his veto. Vetoing spending on veterans was particularly tough, but Coolidge believed that it was wrong for the government to favor interest groups, even much-loved groups. The farm lobby, powerful even then, expected a president from Vermont to support agricultural subsidy. After all, Vermonters know privation firsthand: the land in Plymouth was scarcely arable, and it was said that the farmers of Vermont "farmed rocks." Yet Coolidge vetoed farm subsidies twice, commenting that it was not up to the government to help an individual group.

The greatest domestic test for a president who advocates federal restraint is humanitarian disaster—a pandemic or a Katrina. In 1927 just such a disaster struck: the Great Mississippi

River Flood, which displaced hundreds of thousands. Coolidge knew that if he went to the flood sites, the political pressure to back broad federal rescue money would be as unstoppable as the river waters. So Coolidge stayed away from the disaster zone, to the disapproval of many, who painted him as cruel or lazy. Senator Thaddeus Caraway of Arkansas, furious at Coolidge's refusal to call an extra session of Congress or authorize a new disaster law, commented icily, "I venture to say that if a similar disaster had affected New England that the president would have had no hesitation in calling an extra session."

The autumn brought to Coolidge an irony of biblical proportion. Disaster *did* affect New England: a second flood inundated Coolidge's own Vermont, destroying the rail lines and dozens of covered bridges, and drowning the lieutenant governor, carried away when he exited his car in Barre. Coolidge agonized—poring over aerial pictures of flooding in his own Windsor County— yet chose to live by example and stayed away. After all, he was president of the United States, not president of Vermont. Some Vermonters understood: "He can't do for his own, you see, more than he did for the others," a citizen told a reporter.

All presidents have flaws. Coolidge's flaw, as that of his party, was his inconsistency on foreign economic policy. U.S. policy at the time was to help other nations by promoting economic growth. But tariffs that Coolidge backed kept European nations from recovering from World War I and hurt developing democracies. The damage of tariff increases that Coolidge permitted to be levied on Cuba would be felt for many decades.

Ultimately, presidents should be judged on their own terms— on whether they achieve what they set out to do. In most areas, Coolidge did achieve what he set out to do. Joblessness in the 1920s stayed low, often below 5 percent. Wages rose. Every year he forced the federal budget down some more, so that when he left office the budget was lower than when he had taken office, a record for a peacetime president. By the time Coolidge left Washington, the national debt had dropped by one-third from its postwar high, assuring American economic primacy in the world.

Economic growth in the Coolidge years averaged 4 percent a year, a level we can only aspire to today. Automobiles and electricity came even to working-class families. Veterans never got bonuses on a scale they sought, but many did get jobs. Many farmers headed for the cities and found lucrative jobs in steel or auto plants. African Americans—some of those brutally displaced by the Great Mississippi River Flood—found jobs in the North. The number of lynchings nationwide dropped. In Coolidge's time, indoor plumbing, a key marker of the escape from poverty, became the rule rather than the exception. Innovators patented new ideas at a rate still admired in the twenty-first century. Because of automation resulting from such innovation, factories could do in five days what they had previously done in six. That meant families got a gift in time as well: Saturday. Thanks to Coolidge, the 1920s, contra progressive historians, were no champagne bubble but a decade to replicate.

AMERICANS RECOGNIZED COOLIDGE'S SUCCESS. The 1924 presidential election was a tough three-party contest. The Progressive Party's Robert La Follette gained nearly 17 percent of the vote. Yet Coolidge not only won in 1924; he pulled an absolute majority of votes, defeating the third party and Democrats combined. In 1928, after failing to persuade Coolidge to run again, the frustrated Republicans nominated his secretary of commerce, Herbert Hoover, who sailed to victory on a plan of "continuation of Coolidge policies."

Coolidge went to elaborate lengths to demonstrate modesty and advance constitutional principles even after the presidency.

The sculptor Borglum, sensing Coolidge's ambivalence at the sight of Rushmore, asked Coolidge to write text about America's Founding that would be included at the Rushmore monument. Coolidge at first agreed but, disliking Borglum's audacious edits of his work, withdrew from the project. When friends and supporters raised funds for a Coolidge Library, the president chose to spend the money not on his own legacy but as a gift to the institution in which his wife, Grace, had long been involved, the Clarke School for the Deaf in Northampton, Massachusetts. As he explicitly states in this book, Coolidge believed former presidents should not live off the federal purse. As a result, there is no federally funded Coolidge Presidential Library. At the Calvin Coolidge Presidential Foundation, we seek to honor the president's intentions and currently operate without federal aid. Still, it is our business—our obligation—to convey Coolidge policies and principles through his person. For a century on, Coolidge ideas have not lost relevance. Quite the contrary: in an age of exploding debt, increasingly centralized government power, and fierce partisan division, Calvin Coolidge offers important insights for citizens and political leaders alike.

There is no better place to begin to take in those insights than in Coolidge's autobiography. This slim volume offers a first glimpse into the expansive Coolidge legacy—modest, determined, virtuous, and, in its way, monumental.

Amity Shlaes is the author of Coolidge, The Forgotten Man, *and* Great Society, *among other books. She chairs the Calvin Coolidge Presidential Foundation.*

Matthew Denhart is president of the Calvin Coolidge Presidential Foundation.

TIMELINE

July 4, 1872   John Calvin Coolidge is born to John Coolidge
                    and Victoria Moor Coolidge in Plymouth
                    Notch, Vermont. A sister, Abigail Gratia
                    (Abbie) Coolidge, is born in 1875.

March 14, 1885   Calvin's mother, Victoria, dies.

1886–1890   Coolidge attends boarding school at Black
                    River Academy in Ludlow, Vermont.

March 6, 1890   Calvin's sister, Abbie, dies at age fourteen,
                    probably of appendicitis.

Autumn 1891   Coolidge enrolls in Amherst College, graduat-
                    ing cum laude in 1895. Though shy, he makes
                    a name for himself on campus as a debater.

September 1895   The Coolidge family decides against law school.
                    Coolidge will "read law," an old common-law

country practice of learning at a firm, at Hammond and Field in Northampton, Massachusetts. He drops "John" from his name, becoming simply "Calvin Coolidge."

1897–1904   Coolidge begins his climb in Bay State law and politics, opening his own law practice and serving in various local political positions, including Republican city ward committeeman, city councilman, city solicitor, clerk of courts of Hampshire County, and Republican city committee chairman for Northampton.

October 4, 1905   Coolidge marries Grace Anna Goodhue, a trainee at the Clarke School for the Deaf. The Coolidges rent half of a two-family home at 21 Massasoit Street in Northampton.

September 7, 1906   A son, John Coolidge, is born to Calvin and Grace.

1906–1909   Coolidge is elected to and serves two terms in the Massachusetts House of Representatives.

April 13, 1908   A second son, Calvin Coolidge Jr., is born to Calvin and Grace.

1909–1911   Coolidge is elected mayor of Northampton and serves two terms.

1911–1915   Coolidge is elected to and serves multiple terms in the Massachusetts senate. An important mentor is Senator W. Murray Crane, who leads the famous paper company Crane's.

February 3, 1913   The Sixteenth Amendment to the U.S. Constitution is ratified, establishing Congress's right to impose a federal income tax.

April 8, 1913   The Seventeenth Amendment to the U.S. Constitution is ratified, allowing voters to cast direct votes for U.S. senators rather than having state legislatures choose a state's representatives to the U.S. Senate.

January 7, 1914   Calvin Coolidge delivers the speech "Have Faith in Massachusetts" on becoming president of the Massachusetts senate. Coolidge advises: "Don't hesitate to be as revolutionary as science. Don't hesitate to be as reactionary as the multiplication table. Don't expect to help the weak by pulling down the strong."

1915–1918   Coolidge is elected lieutenant governor of Massachusetts and serves two terms.

November 5, 1918   Coolidge is elected governor of Massachusetts at age forty-six.

November 11, 1918   Armistice Day marks the end of the First World War.

January 16, 1919   The Eighteenth Amendment to the U.S. Constitution is ratified, establishing the prohibition of alcohol in the United States.

June 4, 1919   The Nineteenth Amendment to the U.S. Constitution is ratified, granting women the right to vote.

September 3, 1919   Governor Coolidge delivers a speech celebrating the 250th anniversary of the settling of Westfield, Massachusetts. He highlights the importance of the U.S. Constitution as a unifying document.

September 1919   The Boston police force breaks its contract and walks out on strike to protest low wages and poor conditions. The move prompts strong action by Governor Coolidge to ensure law and order. Coolidge calls out the Massachusetts State Guard and fires the policemen. Coolidge's handling of the crisis catapults him to national prominence.

November 1919   Coolidge is reelected governor of Massachusetts.

June 12, 1920   With the United States mired in debt from World War I, burdened by high taxes, and vying with Britain to become the world's leading economic power, the Republican National Convention nominates candidates for president and vice president who emphasize economic programs to sustain prosperity: Warren Harding and Calvin Coolidge, respectively. The Harding-Coolidge campaign runs with the promise of less uncertain business conditions, lower taxes, budgetary rigor, and "a return to normalcy."

November 2, 1920   Harding is elected president of the United States; Coolidge is elected vice president. The Coolidges move to Washington, D.C., and take up residence in the New Willard Hotel.

June 10, 1921   The Budget and Accounting Act of 1921 gives
                       the president his own research /staff via the
                       new Bureau of the Budget, and wider author-
                       ity to manage the federal budget. The new
                       tools make it easier for Presidents Harding and
                       Coolidge to restrain congressional spending.

August 10, 1922   Vice President Coolidge delivers the speech
                       "Limitations of the Law" in San Francisco.
                       Coolidge says, "There is no justification
                       for public interference with purely private
                       concerns."

August 3, 1923   The unexpected news of President Harding's
                       death reaches the Coolidges while they vaca-
                       tion in Plymouth Notch. Coolidge is sworn
                       into the office of president by his father, John
                       Coolidge, a notary public. The humility dis-
                       played in this event becomes a hallmark of the
                       Coolidge presidency.

1924   Sales of a new apparatus, the radio, reach
                       $350 million, an exponential increase from the
                       level at the start of the decade.

May 15, 1924   Coolidge vetoes a bill to give bonuses to vet-
                       erans of the First World War, fearing that the
                       bonuses will overstretch the budget. In his veto
                       message, Coolidge writes, "The gratitude of the
                       nation to these veterans cannot be expressed
                       in dollars and cents." He continues: "Patriotism
                       can neither be bought nor sold. It is not hire
                       and salary. It is not material, but spiritual." Con-
                       gress later overrides Coolidge's veto.

May 24, 1924	With overwhelming bipartisan support, Congress passes the Johnson-Reed Immigration Act, halting most immigration from eastern and southern Europe, as well as from Japan. Coolidge signs the bill into law, noting his regret over, in particular, the Japanese exclusion provision, which he calls "deplorable."
June 2, 1924	Coolidge signs legislation cutting tax rates and promises to "bend his energies" for further cuts in future legislation.
June 2, 1924	Coolidge signs the Indian Citizenship Act, which declares that "all non-citizen Indians born within the territorial limits of the United States be, and they are hereby, declared to be citizens of the United States."
June 6, 1924	Coolidge delivers the commencement speech at Howard University in Washington, D.C., a historically black college.
July 7, 1924	Coolidge's younger son, Calvin Jr., dies of sepsis from a blister sustained while playing tennis on the White House court.
October 26, 1924	Coolidge delivers his "Discriminating Benevolence" speech over the phone from the White House to an audience of the Federation of Jewish Philanthropic Societies of New York City, remarking, "I regard a good budget as among the noblest monuments of virtue." He commends the community leaders, telling them, "I want you to know that I feel you are making

good citizens, that you are strengthening the government, that you are demonstrating the supremacy of the spiritual life and helping establish the Kingdom of God on earth."

November 4, 1924   Coolidge is elected president in a landslide, earning an absolute majority of the popular vote in a three-way race with Democrat John W. Davis and Progressive Party candidate Robert La Follette.

November 1924   Macy's holds its first Thanksgiving Day Parade.

1925   Sears, Roebuck opens its first direct retail store, expanding to more than 300 stores nationwide by the end of the decade. Chain stores spring up widely during the 1920s as consumers become more confident in the prosperous economy.

October 6, 1925   In Omaha, Nebraska, Coolidge delivers the speech "Toleration and Liberalism," a call for unity among all citizens, whatever their ethnic background. Coolidge says: "Whether one traces his Americanism back three centuries to the *Mayflower*, or three years to the steerage, is not half so important as whether his Americanism of today is real and genuine. No matter by what various crafts we came here, we are all now in the same boat."

February 1926   Coolidge signs the Revenue Act of 1926, decreasing the top marginal income tax rate to 25 percent.

March 18, 1926   Coolidge's father, Colonel John Coolidge, dies
                      in Plymouth Notch.

May 1926   A general strike paralyzes British industry and
                      political life after mine owners threaten to cut
                      pay and increase hours. Troubled Britain increas-
                      ingly provides a contrast to the United States,
                      where productivity gains are strong enough
                      that industry is shifting from the traditional six-
                      day workweek to a new five-day-a-week model,
                      with paid vacations becoming more common.
                      American economic primacy is solidifying.

July 5, 1926   Coolidge delivers "The Inspiration of the Dec-
                      laration" speech in Philadelphia to celebrate
                      the 150th anniversary of the signing of the
                      Declaration of Independence. He asserts: "If
                      all men are created equal, that is final. If they
                      are endowed with inalienable rights, that is
                      final. If governments derive their just powers
                      from the consent of the governed, that is final.
                      No advance, no progress can be made beyond
                      these propositions."

February 25, 1927   Coolidge vetoes the McNary-Haugen Farm
                      Relief Act, by which the federal govern-
                      ment would fix agricultural prices and then
                      buy farmers' products at those artificially high
                      prices.

Spring 1927   The Mississippi River floods to unprecedented
                      levels, displacing hundreds of thousands of
                      people in Mississippi, Arkansas, and Louisiana.
                      Like President Grover Cleveland before him,

Coolidge refrains from traveling to flood sites, wary of setting a precedent of large-scale federal rescues during natural disasters.

Fall 1927

Flooding in Coolidge's own Vermont causes damage and destruction throughout the state. As he did earlier in the year after the Mississippi flood, the president stays away from the disaster site and pursues a restrained federal response.

August 2, 1927

Coolidge announces, "I do not choose to run for President in nineteen twenty eight," via handwritten slips of paper given to reporters in Rapid City, South Dakota, the site of the 1927 Summer White House.

October 20, 1927

The Ford Model A comes to market, the second mass model produced by the Ford Motor Company. The previous Model T automobile was available for eighteen years.

May 23, 1928

Coolidge vetoes the McNary-Haugen Act for a second time.

May 26, 1928

Coolidge is presented with a bill to use federal resources to dam the Tennessee River to generate energy. The president uses the pocket veto to block the bill.

September 21, 1928

Coolidge delivers a brief speech at Bennington, fondly proclaiming, "Vermont is a state I love." The speech follows two days of touring the Green Mountain State to see the progress of recovery efforts after the previous year's devastating flood.

November 6, 1928   Coolidge's secretary of commerce, Herbert Hoover, is elected president of the United States.

January 17, 1929   Coolidge signs the Kellogg-Briand Pact into law. Under the treaty, sixty-two nations agree to renounce war as a means of international policy.

March 4, 1929   Coolidge leaves office, having balanced the federal budget every year while president. Coolidge's budget efforts have resulted in a significant reduction in the size of the national debt and a decrease in overall federal spending. The national debt falls by a third during the Coolidge presidency, from $22.3 billion in 1923 to $16.9 billion in 1929. The Coolidges return via rail to Northampton.

May 1929   *The Autobiography of Calvin Coolidge* is published for the first time.

Autumn 1929   The stock market crashes.

1930   The Coolidges move to a more private Northampton home, the Beeches.

June 1930–June 1931 Coolidge writes a syndicated daily newspaper column, "Calvin Coolidge Says."

1932   Unemployment rises past 20 percent. New York governor Franklin Delano Roosevelt is elected

　　　　　　　　　　U.S. president. Roosevelt's "New Deal" prom-
　　　　　　　　　　ises active government and progressivism.

January 5, 1933　　Coolidge dies at age sixty at the Beeches. The
　　　　　　　　　　Wall Street Journal comments that although
　　　　　　　　　　the New Deal might undo some of Coolidge's
　　　　　　　　　　achievements, "in due time, the good fortune
　　　　　　　　　　of the United States to have had such a man as
　　　　　　　　　　Calvin Coolidge in just the years he filled that
　　　　　　　　　　office will be more clearly realized than it has
　　　　　　　　　　yet been."

September 16, 1956　The Forbes Library in Northampton, which
　　　　　　　　　　possesses many of the papers and other ephem-
　　　　　　　　　　era related to Calvin Coolidge, dedicates the
　　　　　　　　　　Calvin Coolidge Memorial Room.

July 8, 1957　　　Former first lady Grace Coolidge dies at age
　　　　　　　　　　seventy-eight.

1960　　　　　　　President Coolidge's son John Coolidge and
　　　　　　　　　　a group of friends and supporters found the
　　　　　　　　　　Coolidge Foundation to preserve the legacy
　　　　　　　　　　of Coolidge's time in office. The founda-
　　　　　　　　　　tion begins a long partnership with the state
　　　　　　　　　　of Vermont at the historic birthplace site in
　　　　　　　　　　Plymouth Notch.

1981　　　　　　　President Ronald Reagan places a portrait of
　　　　　　　　　　Coolidge in the White House Cabinet Room.

May 31, 2000　　　Coolidge's elder son, John Coolidge, dies at age
　　　　　　　　　　ninety-three.

THE AUTOBIOGRAPHY OF
CALVIN COOLIDGE

1

SCENES OF MY CHILDHOOD

T he town of Plymouth lies on the easterly slope of the Green Mountains, about twenty miles west of the Connecticut River and somewhat south of the central part of Vermont. This part of the state is made up of a series of narrow valleys and high hills, some of which rank as mountains that must reach an elevation of at least twenty-five hundred feet.

Its westerly boundary is along the summit of the main range to where it falls off into the watershed of Lake Champlain and the St. Lawrence River. At one point a little rill comes down a mountain until it strikes a rock, where it divides, part running north into the Ottauquechee and part south into the Black River, both of which later turn easterly to reach the Connecticut.

In its natural state this territory was all covered with evergreen and hardwood trees. It had large deposits of limestone, occasionally mixed with marble, and some granite. There were sporadic outcroppings of iron ore, and the sands of some of the streams showed considerable traces of gold. The soil was hard and rocky, but when cultivated supported a good growth of vegetation.

During colonial times this region lay in an unbroken wilderness, until the coming of the French and Indian War, when a military road was cut through under the direction of General Amherst, running from Charlestown, New Hampshire, to Fort Ticonderoga, New York. This line of march lay through the south part of the town, crossing the Black River at the head of the two beautiful lakes and running over the hill towards the valley of the Otter Creek.

When settlers began to come in around the time of the Revolution, the grandfather of my grandfather, Captain John Coolidge, located a farm near the height of land westward from the river along this military road, where he settled in about 1780.

He had served in the Revolutionary army and may have learned of this region from some of his comrades who had known it in the old French wars, or who had passed over it in the campaign against Burgoyne, which culminated at Saratoga.

He had five children and acquired five farms, so that each of his descendants was provided with a homestead. His oldest son Calvin came into possession of the one which I now own, where it is said that Captain John spent his declining years. He lies buried beside his wife in the little neighborhood cemetery not far distant.

The early settlers of Plymouth appear to have come mostly from Massachusetts, though some of them had stopped on the way in New Hampshire. They were English Puritan stock, and their choice of a habitation stamps them with a courageous pioneering spirit.

Their first buildings were log houses, the remains of which were visible in some places in my early boyhood, though they had long since been given over to the sheltering of domestic animals. The town must have settled up with considerable rapidity, for as early as 1840 it had about fourteen hundred inhabitants scattered

about the valleys and on the sides of the hills, which the mountains divided into a considerable number of different neighbor-
hoods, each with a well-developed local community spirit.

As time went on, much land was cleared of forest, very
substantial buildings of wood construction were erected, saw
mills and grist mills were located along the streams, and the
sale of lumber and lime, farm products and domestic animals,
brought considerable money into the town, which was laid out
for improvements or found its way into the country store. It was
a hard but wholesome life, under which the people suffered
many privations and enjoyed many advantages, without any clear
realization of the existence of either one of them.

They were a hardy self-contained people. Most of them are
gone now and their old homesteads are reverting to the wilderness. They went forth to conquer where the trees were thicker,
the fields larger, and the problems more difficult. I have seen
their descendants scattered all over the country, especially in
the middle west, and as far south as the Gulf of Mexico and
westward to the Pacific slope.

It was into this community that I was born on the 4th day
of July, 1872. My parents then lived in a five room, story and
a half cottage attached to the post office and general store, of
which my father was the proprietor. While they intended to
name me for my father, they always called me Calvin, so the
John became discarded.

Our house was well shaded with maple trees and had a yard
in front enclosed with a picket fence, in which grew a mountain
ash, a plum tree, and the customary purple lilac bushes. In the
summertime my mother planted her flower bed there.

Her parents, who were prosperous farmers, lived in the large
house across the road, which had been built for a hotel and still
has the old hall in it where public dances were held in former

days and a spacious corner on the front side known as the bar room, indicating what had been sold there before my grandfather Moor bought the premises. On an adjoining farm, about sixty-five rods distant,* lived my grandfather and grandmother Coolidge. Within view were two more collections of farm buildings, three dwelling houses with their barns, a church, a school house and a blacksmith shop. A little out of sight dwelt the local butter tub maker and beyond him the shoemaker.

This locality was known as The Notch, being situated at the head of a valley in an irregular bowl of hills. The scene was one of much natural beauty, of which I think the inhabitants had little realization, though they all loved it because it was their home and were always ready to contend that it surpassed all the surrounding communities and compared favorably with any other place on earth.

My sister Abbie was born in the same house in April, 1875. We lived there until 1876, when the place was bought across the road, which had about two acres of land with a house and a number of barns and a blacksmith shop. About it were a considerable number of good apple trees. I think the price paid was $375. Almost at once the principal barn was sold for $100, to be moved away. My father was a good trader.

Some repairs were made on the inside, and black walnut furniture was brought from Boston to furnish the parlor and sitting room. It was a plain square-sided house with a long ell, to which the horse barn was soon added. The outside has since been remodeled and the piazza built. A young woman was always employed to do the house work. Whatever was needed never failed to be provided.

---

* A rod is a measure of distance equal to 16.5 feet. This measure was much more common in the late nineteenth and early twentieth centuries than it is today.

While in theory I was always urged to work and to save, in practice I was permitted to do my share of playing and wasting. My playthings often lay in the road to be run over, and my ball game often interfered with my filling the wood box. I have been taken out of bed to do penance for such derelictions.

My father, John Calvin Coolidge, ran the country store. He was successful. The annual rent of the whole place was $40. I have heard him say that his merchandise bills were about $10,000 yearly. He had no other expenses. His profits were about $100 per month on the average, so he must have sold on a very close margin.

He trusted nearly everybody, but lost a surprisingly small amount. Sometimes people he had not seen for years would return and pay him the whole bill.

He went to Boston in the spring and fall to buy goods. He took the midnight train from Ludlow when they did not have sleeping cars, arriving in the city early in the morning, which saved him his hotel bill.

He was a good business man, a very hard worker, and did not like to see things wasted. He kept the store about thirteen years and sold it to my mother's brother, who became a prosperous merchant.

In addition to his business ability my father was very skillful with his hands. He worked with a carriage maker for a short time when he was young, and the best buggy he had for twenty years was one he made himself. He had a complete set of tools, ample to do all kinds of building and carpenter work. He knew how to lay bricks and was an excellent stone mason.

Following his sale of the store about the time my grandfather died, besides running the farm, he opened the old blacksmith shop which stood upon the place across the road to which we had moved. He hired a blacksmith at $1 per day, who was a large-framed powerful man with a black beard, said to be sometimes quarrelsome.

I have seen him unaided throw a refractory horse to the ground when it objected to being shod. But he was always kind to me, letting me fuss around the shop, leaving his own row to do three or four hills for me so that I could more easily keep up with the rest of the men in hoeing time, or favoring me in some way in the hay field as he helped on the farm in busy times.

He always pitched the hay on to the ox cart and I raked after. If I was getting behind he slowed up a little. He was a big-hearted man. I wish I could see that blacksmith again. The iron work for farm wagons and sleds was fashioned and put on in the shop, oxen and horses brought there for shoeing, and metal parts of farm implements often repaired. My father seemed to like to work in the shop, but did not go there much except when a difficult piece of work was required, like welding a broken steel section rod of a mowing machine, which had to be done with great precision or it would break again.

He kept tools for mending shoes and harnesses and repairing water pipes and tinware. He knew how to perform all kinds of delicate operations on domestic animals. The lines he laid out were true and straight, and the curves regular. The work he did endured.

If there was any physical requirement of country life which he could not perform, I do not know what it was. From watching him and assisting him, I gained an intimate knowledge of all this kind of work.

It seems impossible that any man could adequately describe his mother. I can not describe mine.

On the side of her father, Hiram Dunlap Moor, she was Scotch with a mixture of Welsh and English. Her mother, Abigail (Franklin) Moor, was chiefly of the old New England stock.

She bore the name of two Empresses, Victoria Josephine. She was of a very light and fair complexion with a rich growth of brown hair that had a glint of gold in it. Her hands and features were regular and finely modeled. The older people always told me how beautiful she was in her youth.

She was practically an invalid ever after I could remember her, but used what strength she had in lavish care upon me and my sister, who was three years younger. There was a touch of mysticism and poetry in her nature which made her love to gaze at the purple sunsets and watch the evening stars.

Whatever was grand and beautiful in form and color attracted her. It seemed as though the rich green tints of the foliage and the blossoms of the flowers came for her in the springtime, and in the autumn it was for her that the mountain sides were struck with crimson and with gold.

When she knew that her end was near she called us children to her bedside, where we knelt down to receive her final parting blessing.

In an hour she was gone. It was her thirty-ninth birthday. I was twelve years old. We laid her away in the blustering snows of March. The greatest grief that can come to a boy came to me. Life was never to seem the same again.*

Five years and forty-one years later almost to a day my sister and my father followed her. It always seemed to me that the boy I lost was her image. They all rest together on the sheltered hillside among five generations of the Coolidge family.

My grandfather, Calvin Galusha Coolidge, died when I was six years old. He was a spare man over six feet tall, of a nature

---

* Coolidge's mother, Victoria, died in 1885, probably of tuberculosis. The Centers for Disease Control and Prevention estimate that tuberculosis was responsible for one out of every seven deaths during this period.

which caused people to confide in him, and of a character which made him a constant choice for public office. His mother and her family showed a marked trace of Indian blood. I never saw her, but he took me one time to see her sister, his very aged aunt, whom we found sitting in the chimney corner smoking a clay pipe.

This was so uncommon that I always remembered it. I thought tobacco was only for men, though I had seen old ladies outside our neighborhood buy snuff at the store.

He was an expert horseman and loved to raise colts and puppies. He kept peacocks and other gay-colored fowl and had a yard and garden filled with scarlet flowers. But he never cared to hunt or fish. He found great amusement in practical jokes and could entice a man into a nest of bees and make him think he went there of his own accord.

He and my grandmother brought up as their own children the boy and girl of his only sister, whose parents died when they were less than two years old. He made them no charge, but managed their inheritance and turned it all over to them with the income, besides giving the boy $800 of his own money when he was eighteen years old, the same as he did my father. He was fond of riding horseback and taught me to ride standing up behind him. Some of the horses he bred and sold became famous. In his mind, the only real, respectable way to get a living was from tilling the soil. He therefore did not exactly approve having his son go into trade.

In order to tie me to the land, in his last sickness he executed a deed to me for life of forty acres, called the Lime Kiln lot, on the west part of his farm, with the remainder to my lineal descendants, thinking that as I could not sell it, and my creditors could not get it, it would be necessary for me to cultivate it. He also gave me a mare colt and a heifer calf, which came of stock that had belonged to his grandfather.

Two days after I was two months old, my father was elected to the state legislature. By a curious coincidence, when my son was the same age I was elected to the same office in Massachusetts. He was reelected twice, the term being two years, and, while he was serving, my grandfather took my mother and me to visit him at Montpelier.

I think I was three years and four months old, but I always remembered the experience. Grandfather carried me to the State House and sat me in the Governor's chair, which did not impress me so much as a stuffed catamount that was in the capital museum. That was the first of the great many journeys which I have since made to legislative halls.

During his last illness he would have me read to him the first chapter of the Gospel of John, which he had read to his grandfather. I could do very well until I came to the word "comprehended," with which I always had difficulty. On taking the oath as President in 1925, I placed my hand on that Book of the Bible in memory of my first reading it.

So far as I know, neither he nor any other members of my family ever entertained any ambitions in my behalf. He evidently wished me to stay on the land. My own wish was to keep store, as my father had done.

They all taught me to be faithful over a few things. If they had any idea that such a training might some day make me a ruler over many things, it was not disclosed to me. It was my father in later years who wished me to enter the law, but when I finally left home for that purpose the parting was very hard for him to bear.

The neighborhood around The Notch was made up of people of exemplary habits. Their speech was clean and their lives were above reproach. They had no mortgages on their farms. If any debts were contracted they were promptly paid. Credit was good and there was money in the savings bank.

The break of day saw them stirring. Their industry continued until twilight. They kept up no church organization, and as there was little regular preaching the outward manifestation of religion through public profession had little opportunity, but they were without exception a people of faith and charity and of good works. They cherished the teachings of the Bible and sought to live in accordance with its precepts.

The conduct of the young people was modest and respectful. For most of the time during my boyhood regular Sunday school classes were held in the church which my grandmother Coolidge superintended until in her advanced years she was superseded by my father. She was a constant reader of the Bible and a devoted member of the church, who daily sought for divine guidance in prayer.*

I stayed with her at the farm much of the time and she had much to do with shaping the thought of my early years. She had a benign influence over all who came in contact with her. The Puritan severity of her convictions was tempered by the sweetness of a womanly charity. There were none whom she ever knew that had not in some way benefited by her kindness.

Her maiden name was Sarah Almeda Brewer. When she married my grandfather she was twenty and he was twenty-eight years old. She was accustomed to tell me that from his experience and observations he had come to have great faith in good blood, and that he chose her for his wife not only because he loved her, but because her family, which he had seen for three generations, were people of ability and character.

While he would have looked upon rank as only pretense, he looked upon merit with great respect. His judgment was

---

* Today visitors who come to Plymouth Notch, Vermont, may visit Union Christian Church and the Coolidge family pew.

vindicated by the fact that more of her kin folks than he could have realized had been and were to become people of merited distinction.

The prevailing dress in our neighborhood was that of the countryside. While my father wore a business suit with a white shirt, collar and cuffs, which he always kept clean, the men generally had colored shirts and outer garments of brown or blue drilling. But they all had good clothes for any important occasions.

I was clad in a gingham shirt with overalls in the summer, when I liked to go barefooted. In the winter these were changed for heavy wool garments and thick cowhide boots, which lasted a year.

My grandmother Coolidge spun woolen yarn, from which she knitted us stockings and mittens. I have seen her weave cloth, and when I was ten years old I had a frock which came from her loom. We had linen sheets and table cloths and woolen bed blankets, which she had spun and woven in earlier days. I have some of them now. My grandfather Coolidge wore a blue woolen frock much of the time, which is a most convenient garment for that region. It is cut like a shirt, going on over the head, with flaps that reach to the knees.

When I went to visit the old home in later years I liked to wear the one he left, with some fine calfskin boots about two sizes too large for me, which were made for him when he went to the Vermont legislature about 1858. When news pictures began to be taken of me there, I found that among the public this was generally supposed to be a makeup costume, which it was not, so I have since been obliged to forego the comfort of wearing it. In public life it is sometimes necessary in order to appear really natural to be actually artificial.

Perhaps some glimpse of these pictures may have caused an English writer to refer to me as a Vermont backwoodsman. I wonder if he describes his King as a Scotchman when he sees him in kilts.

To those of his country who remember that Burgoyne sent home a dispatch saying that the Green Mountains were the abode of the most warlike race on the continent, who hung like a thunder cloud on his left—which was fully borne out by what they helped to do to him at Bennington and Saratoga—I presume the term of Vermont backwoodsman still carries the implication of reproach. But in this country it is an appellation which from General Ethan Allen to Admiral George Dewey has not been without some distinction.*

While the form of government under which the Plymouth people lived was that of a republic, it had a strong democratic trend. The smallest unit was then the school district. Early in my boyhood the women were given a vote on school questions in both the district and town meetings.

The district meeting was held in the evening at the school house each year. The officers were chosen and the rate of the school tax was fixed by popular vote. The board and room of the teacher for two-week periods was then assigned to the lowest bidders. The rates ran from about fifty cents each week in the summer to as high as $1.25 in the winter.

---

* Coolidge notes that during America's early days, Vermont was thought of as the frontier. Vermont was not among the thirteen original colonies; in fact, it was an independent republic from 1777 until statehood in 1791. Leaders such as Ethan Allen earned respect for their independent spirit and willingness to defend their principles and way of life, even in the cold climate of the Green Mountains. Coolidge praised these same qualities throughout his life, saying of Vermonters in a famous speech at Bennington in 1928, "They are a race of pioneers who have almost beggared themselves in the service of others." Coolidge concluded, "If the spirit of Liberty should vanish from other parts of our Union and the support of our institutions should languish, it could all be replenished from the generous store held by the people of the brave little state of Vermont."

The town officers were chosen annually at the March meeting. Here again the rate of taxes was fixed by popular vote. The bonded debt was rather large, coming down, as I was told, from expenses during the war and the costs of reconstructing roads and bridges after the disastrous freshet of 1869.*

The more substantial farmers wanted to raise a large tax to reduce the debt. I noticed my father did not vote on this subject and I inquired his reason. He said that while he could afford to pay a high rate, he did not wish to place so large a burden on those who were less able, and so was leaving them to make their own decision.

In those days there were about two hundred and fifty qualified voters, not over twenty-five of which were Democrats, and the rest Republicans. They had their spirited contests in their elections, but not along party lines.

One of the patriarchs of the town, who was a Democrat, served many years as Moderator by unanimous choice. He was a man of sound common sense and an excellent presiding officer, but without much book learning.

When he read that part of the call for the meeting which recited that it was to act "on the following questions, *viz.*," he always read it "to act upon the following questions, *vizley.*" This caused him to be referred to at times by the irreverent as Old Vizley.

I was accustomed to carry apples and popcorn balls to the

---

* Here Coolidge refers to the burdens that the public bore after the Civil War and after floods such as the "freshet of 1869." Memories of such crises shaped Coolidge's attitude toward government response to natural disasters. In 1927, the year of the Great Mississippi River Flood and a disastrous flood in Vermont, Coolidge did not personally visit the affected areas. Rather, he looked to support the efforts of state and local authorities and called on Americans to assist their fellow citizens through private charity.

town meetings to sell, mainly because my grandmother said my father had done so when he was a boy, and I was exceedingly anxious to grow up to be like him.

On the even years in September came the Freemen's meeting. This was a state election, at which the town representative to the legislature was chosen. They also voted for county and state officers and for a Representative to the Congress, and on each fourth year for Presidential electors.* I attended all of these meetings until I left home and followed them with interest for many of the succeeding years.

Careful provision was made for the administration of justice through local authorities. Those charged with petty crimes and misdemeanors were brought before one of the five Justices of the Peace, who had power to try and sentence with or without calling a jury. He also had a like jurisdiction in civil matters of a small amount.

The more important cases, criminal and civil, went to the County Court which sat in the neighboring town of Woodstock in May and December. My father was nearly all his life a Constable or a Deputy Sheriff, and sometimes both, with power to serve civil and criminal process, so that he arrested those charged with crime and brought them before the Justice for trial.

Unless it would keep me out of school, he would take me with him when attending before the local justices or when he went to the opening session of the County Court. Before him my grandfather had held the same positions, so that together

---

* Coolidge's precision, as when he notes that citizens vote for "presidential electors," reflects his respect for the U.S. Constitution and America's structure of government. The sculptor who created the mighty busts of the presidents at Mount Rushmore, Gutzon Borglum, asked Coolidge to supply text to be etched into granite. When Borglum attempted to rewrite the former president's language about the Constitution, Coolidge withdrew from the project.

they were the peace officers most of the time in our town for nearly seventy-five years.

In addition to this they often settled the estates of deceased persons and acted as guardian of minors. This business was transacted in the Probate Court, where I often went.

My father was at times a Justice of the Peace and always had a commission as notary public. This enabled him to take the acknowledgment of deeds, which he knew how to draw, and administer oaths necessary to pension papers which he filled out for old soldiers usually without charge, or to take affidavits required on any other instruments.

In my youth he was also always engaged in the transaction of all kinds of town business, being constantly elected for that purpose. He was painstaking, precise and very accurate, and had such wide experience that the lawyers of the region knew they could rely on him to serve papers in difficult cases and make returns that would be upheld by the courts.

This work gave him such a broad knowledge of the practical side of the law that people of the neighborhood were constantly seeking his advice, to which I always listened with great interest. He always counseled them to resist injustice and avoid unfair dealing, but to keep their agreements, meet their obligations and observe strict obedience to the law.

By reason of what I saw and heard in my early life, I came to have a good working knowledge of the practical side of government. I understood that it consisted of restraints which the people had imposed upon themselves in order to promote the common welfare.

As I went about with my father when he collected taxes, I knew that when taxes were laid some one had to work to earn the money to pay them. I saw that a public debt was a burden on all the people in a community, and while it was necessary to meet the needs of a disaster it cost much in interest and ought to be retired as soon as possible.*

After the winter work of laying in a supply of wood had been done, the farm year began about the first of April with the opening of the maple-sugar season. This was the most interesting of all the farm operations to me.

With the coming of the first warm days we broke a road through the deep snow into the sugar lot, tapped the trees, set the buckets, and brought the sap to the sugar house, where in a heater and pans it was boiled down into syrup to be taken to the house for sugaring off. We made eight hundred to two thousand pounds, according to the season.

After that the fences had to be repaired where they had been broken down by the snow, the cattle turned out to pasture, and the spring planting done. Then came sheep-shearing time, which was followed by getting in the hay, harvesting and threshing of the grain, cutting and husking the corn, digging the potatoes and picking the apples. Just before Thanksgiving the poultry had to be dressed for market, and a little later the fattened hogs were butchered and the meat salted down. Early in the winter a beef creature was slaughtered.

The work of the farm was done by the oxen, except running the mowing machine and horse rake. I early learned to drive oxen and used to plow with them alone when I was twelve years old. Of course, there was the constant care of the domestic animals, the milking of the cows, and taking them to and from pasture, which was especially my responsibility.

We had husking bees, apple-paring bees and singing schools

---

* The experience of watching the village of Plymouth Notch levy and collect taxes gave Coolidge an unusual awareness of the trade-offs involved in taxation. He saw that greater taxes meant less money for citizens to use to support themselves and their families.

in the winter. There were parties for the young folks and an occasional dramatic exhibition by local talent. Not far away there were some public dances, which I was never permitted to attend.

Some time during the summer we usually went to the circus, often rising by three o'clock so as to get there early. In the autumn we visited the county fair. The holidays were all celebrated in some fashion.

Of course, the Fourth of July meant a great deal to me, because it was my birthday. The first one I can remember was when I was four years old. My father took me fishing in the meadow brook in the morning. I recall that I fell in the water, after which we had a heavy thundershower, so that we both came home very wet. Usually there was a picnic celebration on that day.

Thanksgiving was a feast day for family reunions at the home of the grandparents. Christmas was a sacrament observed with the exchange of gifts, when the stockings were hung, and the spruce tree was lighted in the symbol of Christian faith and love. While there was plenty of hard work, there was no lack of pleasurable diversion.

When the work was done for the day, it was customary to drop into the store to get the evening mail and exchange views on topics of interest. A few times I saw there Attorney General John G. Sargent with his father, who was a much respected man.*

A number of those who came had followed Sheridan, been with Meade at Gettysburg, and served under Grant, but they

---

* John G. Sargent of Ludlow, Vermont, served as the Windsor County state's attorney (1898–1900) and as the attorney general for Vermont (1908–1912). In 1925 the U.S. Senate failed to confirm Coolidge's nominee, Charles Warren, to the sensitive post of U.S. attorney general. Coolidge then turned to his family ally, nominating Sargent for the post. Sargent was confirmed and served as attorney general for the remainder of the Coolidge administration.

seldom volunteered any information about it. They were not talkative and took their military service in a matter of fact way, not as anything to brag about but merely as something they did because it ought to be done.

They drew no class distinctions except towards those who assumed superior airs. Those they held in contempt. They held strongly to the doctrine of equality. Whenever the hired man or the hired girl wanted to go anywhere they were always understood to be entitled to my place in the wagon, in which case I remained at home. This gave me a very early training in democratic ideas and impressed upon me very forcibly the dignity and power, if not the superiority of labor.

It was all a fine atmosphere in which to raise a boy. As I look back on it I constantly think how clean it was. There was little about it that was artificial. It was all close to nature and in accordance with the ways of nature. The streams ran clear. The roads, the woods, the fields, the people—all were clean. Even when I try to divest it of the halo which I know always surrounds the past, I am unable to create any other impression than that it was fresh and clean.

We had some books, but not many. Mother liked poetry and read some novels. Father had no taste for books, but always took and read a daily paper. My grandfather Moor read books and papers, so that he was a well-informed man.

My grandmother Coolidge liked books and besides a daily Chapter in the Bible read aloud to me "The Rangers or the Tory's Daughter" and "The Green Mountain Boys," which were both stories of the early settlers of Vermont during the Revolutionary period. She also had two volumes entitled "Washington and His Generals," and other biographies which I read myself at an early age with a great deal of interest.

At home there were numerous law books. In this way I

grew up with a working knowledge of the foundations of my state and nation and a taste for history.

My education began with a set of blocks which had on them the Roman numerals and the letters of the alphabet. It is not yet finished. As I played with them and asked my mother what they were, I came to know them all when I was three years old. I started to school when I was five.

The little stone school house which had unpainted benches and desks wide enough to seat two was attended by about twenty-five scholars. Few, if any, of my teachers reached the standard now required by all public schools. They qualified by examination before the town superintendent. I first took this examination and passed it at the age of thirteen and my sister Abbie passed it and taught a term of school in a neighboring town when she was twelve years old.

My teachers were young women from neighboring communities, except sometimes when a man was employed for the winter term. They were all intelligent, of good character, and interested in their work. I do not feel that the quality of their instruction was in any way inferior. The common school subjects were taught, with grammar and United States history, so that when I was thirteen I had mastered them all and went to Black River Academy, at Ludlow.

That was one of the greatest events of my life. The packing and preparation for it required more time and attention than collecting my belongings in preparation for leaving the White House. I counted the hours until it was time to go.

My whole outfit went easily into two small handbags, which lay on the straw in the back of the traverse sleigh beside the fatted calf that was starting to market. The winter snow lay on the ground. The weather was well below freezing. But in my eagerness these counted for nothing.

I was going where I would be mostly my own master. I was casting off what I thought was the drudgery of farm life, symbolized by the cowhide boots and every-day clothing which I was leaving behind, not realizing what a relief it would be to return to them in future years. I had on my best clothes and wore shoes with rubbers, because the village had sidewalks.

I did not know that there were mental and moral atmospheres more monotonous and more contaminating than anything in the physical atmosphere of country life. No one could have made me believe that I should never be so innocent or so happy again.

As we rounded the brow of the hill the first rays of the morning sun streamed over our backs and lighted up the glistening snow ahead. I was perfectly certain that I was traveling out of the darkness into the light.

We have much speculation over whether the city or the country is the better place to bring up boys. I am prejudiced in behalf of the country, but I should have to admit that much depends on the parents and the surrounding neighborhood. We felt the cold in winter and had many inconveniences, but we did not mind them because we supposed they were the inevitable burdens of existence.

It would be hard to imagine better surroundings for the development of a boy than those which I had. While a wider breadth of training and knowledge could have been presented to me, there was a daily contact with many new ideas, and the mind was given sufficient opportunity thoroughly to digest all that came to it.

Country life does not always have breadth, but it has depth. It is neither artificial nor superficial, but is kept close to the realities.

While I can think of many pleasures we did not have, and many niceties of culture with which we were unfamiliar, yet if I had the power to order my life anew I would not dare to change that period of it. If it did not afford me the best that there was, it abundantly provided the best that there was for me.

2

SEEKING AN EDUCATION

O ne of the sages of New England is reported to have declared that the education of a child should begin several generations before it is born. No doubt it does begin at a much earlier period and we enter life with a heritage that reaches back through the ages. But we do not choose our ancestors. When we come into the world the gate of gifts is closed behind us. We can do nothing about it. So far as each individual is concerned all he can do is to take the abilities he has and make the most of them. His power over the past is gone. His power over the future depends on what he does with himself in the present. If he wishes to live and progress he must work.

During early childhood the inspiration for anything like mental discipline comes almost entirely from the outside. It is supplied by the parents and teachers. It was not until I left home in February of 1886 that I could say I had much thought of my own about getting an education. Thereafter I began to be more dependent on myself and assume more and more self-direction.

What I studied was the result of my own choice. Instead of seeking to direct me, my father left me to decide. But when I had selected a course he was always solicitous to see that I diligently applied myself to it.

Going away to school was my first great adventure in life. I shall never forget the impression it made on me. It was so deep and remains so vivid that whenever I have started out on a new enterprise a like feeling always returns to me. It was the same when I went to college, when I left home to enter the law, when I began a public career in Boston, when I started for Washington to become Vice-President and finally when I was called to the White House. Going to the Academy meant a complete break with the past and entering a new and untried field, larger and more alluring than the past, among unknown scenes and unknown people.

In the spring of 1886 Black River Academy had just celebrated its fiftieth anniversary. While it had some distinguished alumni, the great body of its former students were the hard-working, every-day people, that made the strength of rural New England. My father and mother and grandmother Coolidge had been there a few terms. While it had a charter of its own, and was independent of the public authorities, it was nevertheless part village high school.* At its head was a principal, who had under him two women assistants. A red brick structure, built

---

* Vermont has a rich history of academy schools that serve local students and boarders from remote villages. In 1868 the Vermont legislature passed a law granting Ludlow pupils free attendance at Black River Academy, though students from surrounding towns—such as Coolidge—paid tuition. Another Black River Academy pupil, a few years behind Coolidge, was Ida May Fuller, who later became the first recipient of monthly recurring Social Security payments. Today Black River Academy operates as a museum only, but many other academies continue to serve students, including St. Johnsbury Academy, where Coolidge studied for a term in 1891 prior to gaining admission to Amherst College.

like a church, with an assembly room and a few recitation rooms made up its entire equipment, so that those who did not live at home boarded in private families about the town of Ludlow. The spring term began in midwinter in order that the girls could be out by the first Monday in May to teach a summer district school and the boys could get home for the season's work on the farm.

For the very few who were preparing for college a classical course was offered in Latin, Greek, history and mathematics, but most of the pupils kept to the Latin Scientific, and the English courses. The student body was about one hundred and twenty-five in number. During my first term I began algebra and finished grammar. For some reason I was attracted to civil government and took that. This was my first introduction to the Constitution of the United States. Although I was but thirteen years old the subject interested me exceedingly. The study of it which I then began has never ceased, and the more I study it the more I have come to admire it, realizing that no other document devised by the hand of man ever brought so much progress and happiness to humanity. The good it has wrought can never be measured.

It was not alone the school with its teachers, its students and courses of study that interested me, but also the village and its people. It all lay in a beautiful valley along the Black River supported on either side by high hills. The tradespeople all knew my father well and he had an intimate acquaintance with the lawyers. Very soon I too knew them all. The chief industry of the town was a woolen mill that always remained a mystery to me. But the lesser activity of the village was a cab shop. I worked there some on Saturdays, so I came to know how toys and baby wagons were made. It was my first acquaintance with the factory system, and my approach to it was that of a wage earner. As I was employed at piece work my wages depended on my own ability, skill and industry. It was a good training. I was beginning to find out what existence meant.

My real academy course began the next fall term when I started to study Latin. In a few weeks I broke my right arm but it did not keep me out of school more than two days. Latin was not difficult for me to translate, but I never became proficient in its composition. Although I continued it until my sophomore year at college the only part of all the course that I found of much interest was the orations of Cicero. These held my attention to such a degree that I translated some of them in later life.

When Greek was begun the next year I found it difficult. It is a language that requires real attention and close application. Among its rewards are the moving poetry of Homer, the marvelous orations of Demosthenes, and in after life an increased power of observation.

Besides the classics we had a course in rhetoric, some ancient history, and a little American literature. Plane geometry completed our mathematics. In the modern languages there was only French.

In some subjects I began with the class when it started to review and so did the work of a term in two weeks. I joined the French class in mid year and made up the work by starting my study at about three o'clock in the morning.

During the long vacations from May until September I went home and worked on the farm. We had a number of horses so that I was able to indulge my pleasure in riding. As no one else in the neighborhood cared for this diversion I had to ride alone. But a horse is much company, and riding over the fields and along the country roads by himself, where nothing interrupts his seeing and thinking, is a good occupation for a boy. The silences of Nature have a discipline all their own.

Of course our school life was not free from pranks. The property of the townspeople was moved to strange places in the night. One morning as the janitor was starting the furnace he heard a loud bray from one of the class rooms. His investigation disclosed the presence there of a domestic animal noted for his long ears and discordant voice. In some way during the night he had been stabled on the second floor. About as far as I deem it prudent to discuss my own connection with these escapades is to record that I was never convicted of any of them and so must be presumed innocent.

The expenses at the Academy were very moderate. The tuition was about seven dollars for each term, and board and room for each week not over three dollars. Oftentimes students hired a room for about fifty cents per week and boarded themselves. In my own case the cost for a school year averaged about one hundred and fifty dollars, which was all paid by my father. Any money I earned he had me put in the savings bank, because he wished me to be informed of the value of money at interest. He thought money invested in that way led to a self-respecting independence that was one of the foundations of good character.

It was about twelve miles from Ludlow to Plymouth. Sometimes I walked home Friday afternoon, but usually my father came for me and brought me back Sunday evening or Monday morning. When this was not done I often staid with the elder sister of my mother, Mrs. Don C. Pollard, who lived about three miles down the river at Proctorsville. This was my Aunt Sarah who is still living. She was wonderfully kind to me and did all she could to take the place of my own mother in affection for me and good influence over me while I was at the Academy and ever after. The sweetness of her nature was a benediction to all who came in contact with her. What men owe to the love and help of good women can never be told.

The Academy had no athletics in those days, as the boys from the farms did not feel the need of such activity. A few games of baseball were played, but no football or track athletics were possible. Games did not interest me much though I had some skill with a bat. I was rather slender and not so tall as many boys of my age.

Those who attended the school from out of town were all there with a real purpose of improving themselves, so that while there was no lack of fun and play they all worked as best they could, for their coming had meant too much sacrifice at home not to be taken seriously. They had come seeking to better their condition in life through what they might learn and the self-discipline they might secure.

The school had much to be desired in organization and equipment, but it possessed a sturdy spirit and a wholesome regard for truth. Of course the student body came from the country and had country ways, but the boys were inspired with a purpose, and the girls with a sweet sincerity which becomes superior to all the affectations of the drawing-room. In them the native capacity for making real men and women remained all unspoiled.

The Presidential election of 1888 created considerable interest among the students. Most of them favored the Republican candidate Benjamin Harrison against the then President Grover Cleveland. When Harrison was elected, two nights were spent parading the streets with drums and trumpets, celebrating the victory.

During most of my course George Sherman was the principal and Miss M. Belle Chellis was the first assistant. I owe much to the inspiration and scholarly direction which they gave to my undergraduate days. They both lived to see me President and sent me letters at the time, though they left the school long ago. It was under their teaching that I first learned of the glory and grandeur of the ancient civilization that grew up around the Mediterranean and in Mesopotamia. Under their guidance I beheld the marvels of old Babylon, I marched with the Ten Thousand of Xenophon, I witnessed the conflict around beleaguered Troy which doomed that proud city to pillage and to flames, I heard the tramp of the invincible legions of Rome, I saw the victorious galleys of the Eternal City carrying destruction to the Carthaginian shore, and I listened to the lofty eloquence of Cicero and the matchless imagery of Homer. They gave me a vision of the world when it was young and showed me how it grew. It seems to me that it is almost impossible for those who have not traveled that road to reach a very clear conception of what the world now means.

It was in this period that I learned something of the thread of events that ran from the Euphrates and the Nile through Athens to the Tiber and thence stretched on to the Seine and the Thames to be carried overseas to the James, the Charles and the Hudson. I found that the English language was generously compounded with Greek and Latin, which it was necessary to know if I was to understand my native tongue. I discovered that our ideas of democracy came from the agora of Greece, and our ideas of liberty came from the forum of Rome. Something of the sequence of history was revealed to me, so that I began to understand the significance of our own times and our own country.

In March of my senior year my sister Abbie died. She was three years my junior but so proficient in her studies that she was but two classes below me in school. She was ill scarcely a week. Several doctors were in attendance but could not save her. Thirty years later one of them told me he was convinced she had appendicitis, which was a disease not well understood in

1890. I went home when her condition became critical and staid beside her until she passed to join our mother. The memory of the charm of her presence and her dignified devotion to the right will always abide with me.*

In the spring of 1890 came my graduation. The class had five boys and four girls. With so small a number it was possible for all of us to take part in the final exercises with orations and essays. The subject that I undertook to discuss was "Oratory in History," in which I dealt briefly with the effect of the spoken word in determining human action.

It had been my thought, as I was but seventeen, to spend a year in some of the larger preparatory schools and then enter a university. But it was suddenly decided that a smaller college would be preferable, so I went to Amherst. On my way there I contracted a heavy cold, which grew worse, interfering with my examinations, and finally sent me home where I was ill for a considerable time.

But by early winter I was recovered, so that I did a good deal of work helping repair and paint the inside of the store building which my father still owned and rented. There was time for much reading and I gave great attention to the poems of Sir Walter Scott. After a few weeks in the late winter at my old school I went to St. Johnsbury Academy for the spring term. Its principal was Dr. Putney, who was a fine drill-master, a very exact scholar, and an excellent disciplinarian. He readily gave me a certificate entitling me to enter Amherst without further examination, which he would never have done if he had not

---

* "She had been the jolly one in the dour Coolidge family," biographer Hendrik Booraem noted in *The Provincial: Calvin Coolidge and His World, 1885–1895*. Two years after Abbie's death, Coolidge wrote in a letter to his father, "We must think of Abbie as a happy day, counting it as a pleasure to have had it but not a sorrow because it could not last forever."

been convinced I was a proficient student. His indorsement of the work I had already done, after having me in his own classes for a term, showed that Black River Academy was not without some merit.

During the summer vacation my father and I went to the dedication of the Bennington Battle Monument. It was a most elaborate ceremony with much oratory followed by a dinner and more speaking, with many bands of music and a long military parade. The public officials of Vermont and many from New York were there. I heard President Harrison, who was the first President I had ever seen, make an address. As I looked on him and realized that he personally represented the glory and dignity of the United States I wondered how it felt to bear so much responsibility and little thought I should ever know.

The fall of 1891 found me back at Amherst taking up my college course in earnest. Much of its social life centered around the fraternities, and although they did not leave me without an invitation to join them it was not until senior year that an opportunity came to belong to one that I wished to accept. It has been my observation in life that, if one will only exercise the patience to wait, his wants are likely to be filled.

My class was rather small, not numbering more than eighty-five in a student body of about four hundred. President Julius H. Seelye, who had led the college for about twenty years with great success as an educator and inspirer of young men, had just retired. He had been succeeded by President Merrill E. Gates, a man of brilliant intellect and fascinating personality though not the equal of his predecessor in directing college policy. But the faculty as a whole was excellent, having many strong men, and some who were preeminent in the educational field.

The college of that day had a very laudable desire to get students, and having admitted them, it was equally alert in striving to keep them and help them get an education, with the result that very few left of their own volition and almost none were dropped for failure in their work. There was no marked exodus at the first examination period, which was due not only to the attitude of the college but to the attitude of the students, who did not go there because they wished to experiment for a few months with college life and be able to say thereafter they had been in college, but went because they felt they had need of an education, and expected to work hard for that purpose until the course was finished. There were few triflers.

A small number became what we called sports, but they were not looked on with favor, and they have not survived. While the class has lost many excellent men besides, yet it seems to be true that unless men live right they die. Things are so ordered in this world that those who violate its law cannot escape the penalty. Nature is inexorable. If men do not follow the truth they cannot live.

My absence from home during my freshman year was more easy for me to bear because I was no longer leaving my father alone. Just before the opening of college he had married Miss Carrie A. Brown, who was one of the finest women of our neighborhood. I had known her all my life. After being without a mother nearly seven years I was greatly pleased to find in her all the motherly devotion that she could have given me if I had been her own son. She was a graduate of Kimball Union Academy and had taught school for some years. Loving books and music she was not only a mother to me but a teacher. For thirty years she watched over me and loved me, welcoming me when I went home, writing me often when I was away, and encouraging me in all my efforts. When at last she sank to rest she had seen me made Governor of Massachusetts and knew I was being considered for the Presidency.

It seems as though good influences had always been coming into my life. Perhaps I have been more fortunate in that respect than others. But while I am not disposed to minimize the amount of evil in the world I am convinced that the good predominates and that it is constantly all about us, ready for our service if only we will accept it.

In the Amherst College of my day a freshman was not regarded as different from the other classes. He wore no distinctive garb, or emblem, and suffered no special indignities. It would not have been judicious for him to appear on the campus with a silk hat and cane, but as none of the other students resorted to that practice this single restriction was not a severe hardship. A cane rush always took place between the two lower classes very early in the fall term, but it was confined within the limits of good-natured sport, where little damage was done beyond a few torn clothes.* If we had undertaken to have a class banquet where the sophomores could reach us, it undoubtedly would have brought on a collision, but when the time came for one we tactfully and silently departed for Westfield, under cover of a winter evening, where we were not found or molested.

It had long been the practice at Amherst to give careful attention to physical culture. It had, I believe, the first college gymnasium in this country. Each student on entering was given a thorough examination, furnished with a chart showing any bodily deficiencies and given personal direction for their removal. The attendance of the whole class was required at the gymnasium drill for four periods each week, and voluntary

---

* Cane rushes were a common tradition among colleges in the nineteenth century. Coolidge alludes to the origins of the tradition: at one time, freshmen were not allowed to carry canes. In the cane rush, freshmen would appear brandishing walking sticks, which the sophomores would try forcibly to remove. In 1900 the Amherst faculty abolished cane rushes, given how rough the contests had become.

work on the floor was always encouraged. We heard a great deal about a sound mind in a sound body.

At the time of my entrance the two college dormitories were so badly out of repair that they were little used. Later they were completely remodeled and became fully occupied. About ten fraternity houses furnished lodgings for most of the upper class men, but the lower class men roomed at private houses. All the students took their meals in private houses, so that there was a general comingling of all classes and all fraternities around the table, which broke up exclusive circles and increased college democracy.

The places of general assembly were for religious worship, which consisted of the chapel exercises at the first morning period each week day, and church service in the morning, with vespers in the late afternoon, on Sundays. Regular attendance at all of these was required. Of course we did not like to go and talked learnedly about the right of freedom of worship, and the bad mental and moral reactions from which we were likely to suffer as a result of being forced to hear scriptural readings, psalm singings, prayers and sermons. We were told that our choice of a college was optional, but that Amherst had been founded by pious men with the chief object of training students to overcome the unbelief which was then thought to be prevalent, that religious instruction was a part of the prescribed course, and that those who chose to remain would have to take it. If attendance on these religious services ever harmed any of the men of my time I have never been informed of it. The good it did I believe was infinite. Not the least of it was the discipline that resulted from having constantly to give some thought to things that young men would often prefer not to consider. If we did not have the privilege of doing what we wanted to do, we had the much greater benefit of doing what we ought to do. It broke down our selfishness, it conquered our resistance, it supplanted impulse, and finally it enthroned reason.

In intercollegiate athletics Amherst stood well. It won its share of trophies on the diamond, the gridiron and the track, but it did not engage in any of the water sports. The games with Williams and Dartmouth aroused the keenest interest, and honors were then about even. But these outside activities were kept well within bounds and were not permitted to interfere with the real work of the college. Pratt Field had just been completed and was well equipped for outdoor sports, while Pratt Gymnasium had every facility for indoor training. These places were well named, for the Pratt boys were very active in athletics. One of them was usually captain of the football team. I remember that in 1892 George D. Pratt, afterwards Conservation Commissioner of the State of New York, led his team to victory against Dartmouth, thirty to two, and a week later kicked ten straight goals in a gale of wind at the championship game with Williams, leaving the score sixty to nothing in favor of Amherst. But both these colleges have since retaliated with a great deal of success.

In these field events I was only an observer, contenting myself with getting exercise by faithful attendance at the class drills in the gymnasium. In these the entire class worked together with dumbbells for most of the time, but they involved sufficient marching about the floor to give a military flavor which I found very useful in later life when I came in contact with military affairs during my public career.

The Presidential election of 1892 came in my sophomore year. I favored the renomination of Harrison and joined the Republican Club of the college, which participated in a torchlight parade, but the unsatisfactory business condition of the country carried the victory to Cleveland.

For nearly two years I continued my studies of Latin and Greek. Ours was the last class that read Demosthenes on the Crown with Professor William S. Tyler, the head of the Greek department, who had been with the college about sixty years. He was a patriarch in appearance with a long beard and flowing white hair.

His reverence for the ancient Greeks approached a religion. It was illustrated by a story, perhaps apocryphal, that one of his sons was sent to theological school, and not wishing to engage in the ministry, wrote his father that the faculty of the school held that Socrates was in hell. Such a reflection on the Greek philosopher so outraged the old man's loyalty that he wrote his son that the school was no place for him and directed him to come home at once.

In spite of his eighty-odd years he put the fire of youth into the translation of those glowing periods of the master orator, which were such eloquent appeals to the patriotism of the Greeks and such tremendous efforts to rouse them to the defense of their country. Those passages of the marvelous oration he said he had loved to read during the Civil War.

My studies of the ancient languages I supplemented with short courses in French, German and Italian.

But I never became very proficient in the languages. I was more successful at mathematics, which I pursued far enough to take calculus. This course was mostly under George D. Olds, who came to teach when we entered to study, which later caused us to adopt him as an honorary member of our class. In time he became President of the College. He had a peculiar power to make figures interesting and knew how to hold the attention and affection of his students. It was under him that we learned of the universal application of the laws of mathematics. We saw the discoveries of Kepler, Descartes, Newton and their associates bringing the entire universe under one law, so that the most distant point of light revealed by the largest reflector marches in harmony with our own planet. We discovered, too, that the same force that rounds a tear-drop holds all the myriad worlds of the universe in a balanced position. We found that we dwelt in the midst of a Unity which was all subject to the same rules of action. My education was making some headway.

In the development of every boy who is going to amount to anything there comes a time when he emerges from his immature ways and by the greater precision of his thought and action realizes that he has begun to find himself. Such a transition finally came to me. It was not accidental but the result of hard work. If I had permitted my failures, or what seemed to me at the time a lack of success, to discourage me I cannot see any way in which I would ever have made progress. If we keep our faith in ourselves, and what is even more important, keep our faith in regular and persistent application to hard work, we need not worry about the outcome.

During my first two years at Amherst I studied hard but my marks were only fair. It needed some encouragement from my father for me to continue. In junior year, however, my powers began to increase and my work began to improve. My studies became more interesting. I found the course in history under Professor Anson D. Morse was very absorbing. His lectures on medieval and modern Europe were inspiring, seeking to give his students not only the facts of past human experience but also their meaning. He was very strong on the political side of history, bringing before us the great figures from Charlemagne to Napoleon with remarkable distinctness, and showing us the influence of the Great Gregory and Innocent III. The work of Abélard and Erasmus was considered, and the important era of Luther and Calvin thoroughly explored.

In due time we crossed the Channel with William the Conqueror and learned how he subdued and solidified the Kingdom of England. The significance of the long struggle with the Crown before the Parliament finally reached a position of independence was disclosed, and the slow growth of a system of liberty under the law, until at last it was firmly established, was carefully explained.* We saw the British Empire rise until it ruled the seas. The brilliance of the statesmanship of the different periods, the rugged character of the patriotic leaders, of Anselm and Simon de Montfort, of Cromwell and the Puritans, who dared to oppose the tyranny of the kings, the growth of learning, the development of commerce, the administration of justice—all these and more were presented for our consideration. Whatever was essential to a general comprehension of European history we had.

But it was when he turned to the United States that Professor Morse became most impressive. He placed particular emphasis on the era when our institutions had their beginning. Washington was treated with the greatest reverence, and a high estimate was placed on the statesmanlike qualities and financial capacity of Hamilton, but Jefferson was not neglected. In spite of his many vagaries it was shown that in saving the nation from the danger of falling under the domination of an oligarchy, and in establishing a firm rule of the people which was forever to remain, he vindicated the soundness of our political institutions. The whole course was a thesis on good citizenship and good government. Those who took it came to a clearer comprehen-

---

* Professor Morse's specialty was the nature of the political party, a topic that also held the attention of the young Coolidge. The "slow growth" of the system of liberty in England, which Coolidge describes here, is in keeping with Coolidge's preference as a political leader for incremental improvement over radical reform.

sion not only of their rights and liberties but of their duties and responsibilities.

The department of public speaking was under Professor Henry A. Frink. He had a strong hold on his students. His work went along with the other work, practically through the four years, beginning with composition and recitation and passing to the preparation and delivery of orations and participation in public debates. The allied subject of rhetoric I took under Professor John F. Genung, a scholarly man who was held in high respect. The courses in biology, chemistry, economics and geology I was not able to pursue, though they all interested me and were taught by excellent men.

Not the least in the educational values of Amherst was its beautiful physical surroundings. While the college buildings of the early nineties were not impressive, the town with its spacious common and fine elm trees was very attractive. It was located on the arch of a slight ridge flanked on the north by Mount Warner and on the south by the Holyoke Range. The east rose over wooded slopes to the horizon, and the west looked out across the meadows of the Connecticut to the spires of Northampton and the Hampshire Hills beyond. Henry Ward Beecher has dwelt with great admiration and affection on the beauties of this region, where he was a student. Each autumn, when the foliage had put on its richest tints, the College set aside Mountain Day to be devoted to the contemplation of the scenery so wonderfully displayed in forest, hill, and dale, before the frosts of winter laid them bare.

It always seemed to me that all our other studies were in the nature of a preparation for the course in philosophy. The head of this department was Charles E. Garman, who was one of the most remarkable men with whom I ever came in contact. He used numerous text books, which he furnished, and many pamphlets that he not only had written but had printed himself on a hand press in his home. These he pledged us to show to no one outside the class, because, being fragmentary, and disclosing but one line of argument which might be entirely demolished in succeeding lessons, they might involve him in some needless controversy. It is difficult to imagine his superior as an educator. Truly he drew men out.

Beginning in the spring of junior year his course extended through four terms. The first part was devoted to psychology, in order to find out the capacity and the limits of the human mind. It was here that we learned the nature of habits and the great advantage of making them our allies instead of our enemies.

Much stress was placed on a thorough mastery and careful analysis of all the arguments presented by the writers on any subject under consideration. Then when it was certain that they were fully understood they were criticized, so that what was unsound was rejected and what was true accepted. We were thoroughly drilled in the necessity of distinguishing between the accidental and the essential. The proper method of presenting a subject and an argument was discussed. We were not only learning about the human mind but learning how to use it, learning how to think. A problem would often be stated and the class left to attempt to find the solution unaided by the teacher. Above all we were taught to follow the truth whithersoever it might lead. We were warned that this would oftentimes be very difficult and result in much opposition, for there would be many who were not going that way, but if we pressed on steadfastly it was sure to yield the peaceable fruits of the mind. It does.

Our investigation revealed that man is endowed with reason, that the human mind has the power to weigh evidence, to distinguish between right and wrong and to know the truth. I should call this the central theme of his philosophy. While the quantity of the truth we know may be small it is the quality that is important. If we really know one truth the quality of our knowledge could not be surpassed by the Infinite.

We looked upon Garman as a man who walked with God. His course was a demonstration of the existence of a personal God, of our power to know Him, of the Divine immanence, and of the complete dependence of all the universe on Him as the Creator and Father "in whom we live and move and have our being." Every reaction in the universe is a manifestation of His presence. Man was revealed as His son, and nature as the hem of His garment, while through a common Fatherhood we are all embraced in a common brotherhood. The spiritual appeal of music, sculpture, painting and all other art lies in the revelation it affords of the Divine beauty.

The conclusions which followed from this position were logical and inescapable. It sets man off in a separate kingdom from all the other creatures in the universe, and makes him a true son of God and a partaker of the Divine nature. This is the warrant for his freedom and the demonstration of his equality. It does not assume all are equal in degree but all are equal in kind. On that precept rests a foundation for democracy that cannot be shaken. It justifies faith in the people.

No doubt there are those who think they can demonstrate that this teaching was not correct. With them I have no argument. I know that in experience it has worked. In time of crisis my belief that people can know the truth, that when it is presented to them they must accept it, has saved me from many of the counsels of expediency. The spiritual nature of men has a power of its own that is manifest in every great emergency from Runnymede to Marston Moor, from the Declaration of Independence to the abolition of slavery.

In ethics he taught us that there is a standard of righteousness, that might does not make right, that the end does not justify the means and that expediency as a working principle is bound to fail. The only hope of perfecting human relationship is in accordance with the law of service under which men are not so solicitous about what they shall get as they are about what they shall give. Yet people are entitled to the rewards of their industry. What they earn is theirs, no matter how small or how great. But the possession of property carries the obligation to use it in a larger service. For a man not to recognize the truth, not to be obedient to law, not to render allegiance to the State, is for him to be at war with his own nature, to commit suicide. That is why "the wages of sin is death." Unless we live rationally we perish, physically, mentally, spiritually.

A great deal of emphasis was placed on the necessity and dignity of work. Our talents are given us in order that we may serve ourselves and our fellow men. Work is the expression of intelligent action for a specified end. It is not industry, but idleness, that is degrading. All kinds of work from the most menial service to the most exalted station are alike honorable. One of the earliest mandates laid on the human race was to subdue the earth. That meant work.

If he was not in accord with some of the current teachings about religion, he gave to his class a foundation for the firmest religious convictions. He presented no mysteries or dogmas and never asked us to take a theory on faith, but supported every position by facts and logic. He believed in the Bible and constantly quoted it to illustrate his position. He divested religion and science of any conflict with each other, and showed that each rested on the common basis of our ability to know the truth.

To Garman was given a power which took his class up into a high mountain of spiritual life and left them alone with God.

In him was no pride of opinion, no atom of selfishness. He was a follower of the truth, a disciple of the Cross, who bore the infirmities of us all. Those who finished his course in the last term of senior year found in their graduating exercises a real commencement, when they would begin their efforts to serve their fellow men in the practical affairs of life. Of course it was not possible for us to accept immediately the results of his teachings or live altogether in accordance with them. I do not think he expected it. He was constantly reminding us that the spirit was willing but the flesh was strong, but that nevertheless, if we would continue steadfastly to think on these things we would be changed from glory to glory through increasing intellectual and moral power. He was right.

To many my report of his course will seem in complete and crude. I am not writing a treatise but trying to tell what I secured from his teaching, and relating what has seemed important in it to me, from the memory I have retained of it, since I began it thirty-five years ago. He expected it to be supplemented. He was fond of referring to it as a mansion not made with hands, incomplete, but sufficient for our spiritual habitation. What he revealed to us of the nature of God and man will stand. Against it "the gates of hell shall not prevail."

As I look back upon the college I am more and more impressed with the strength of its faculty, with their power for good. Perhaps it has men now with a broader preliminary training, though they then were profound scholars, perhaps it has men of keener intellects though they then were very exact in their reasoning, but the great distinguishing mark of all of them was that they were men of character. Their words carried conviction because we were compelled to believe in the men who uttered them. They had the power not merely to advise but literally to instruct their students.

In accordance with custom our class chose three of its members by popular vote to speak at the commencement. To me was assigned the grove oration, which according to immemorial practice deals with the record of the class in a witty and humorous way. While my effort was not without some success I very soon learned that making fun of people in a public way was not a good method to secure friends, or likely to lead to much advancement, and I have scrupulously avoided it.

In the latter part of my course my scholarship had improved, so that I was graduated *cum laude*.

After my course was done I went home to do a summer's work on the farm, which was to be my last. I had decided to enter the law and expected to attend a law school, but one of my classmates wrote me late in the summer that there was an opportunity to go into the office of Hammond and Field at Northampton, so I applied to them and was accepted. After I had been there a few days a most courteous letter came from the Honorable William P. Dillingham requesting me to call on him at Montpelier and indicating he would take me into his office.* He recalled the circumstance when I found him in the Senate after I became Vice President. But I had already reverted to Massachusetts, where my family had lived for one hundred and fifty years before their advent into Vermont. Had his letter reached me sooner probably it would have changed the whole course of my life.

---

* William P. Dillingham served as governor of Vermont and later as U.S. senator representing Vermont. Under Dillingham's chairmanship, the U.S. Immigration Commission produced what became known as the Dillingham Report, which helped fuel the drive for immigration restriction and the eventual passage of the Johnson-Reed Act in 1924. Dillingham died in July 1923; Porter H. Dale, who was present in Plymouth Notch for Coolidge's "Homestead Inauguration," completed Dillingham's term in the Senate.

Northampton was the county seat and a quiet but substantial town, with pleasant surroundings and fine old traditions reaching back beyond Jonathan Edwards. It was just recovering from the depression of 1893, preparing to eliminate its grade crossings and starting some new industries that would add to the business it secured from Smith College, which was a growing institution with many hundreds of students.

The senior member of the law firm was John C. Hammond, who was considered the leader of the Hampshire Bar. He was a lawyer of great learning and wide business experience, with a remarkable ability in the preparation of pleadings and an insight that soon brought him to the crucial point of a case. He was massive and strong rather than elegant, and placed great stress on accuracy. He presented a cause in court with ability and skill. The junior member was Henry P. Field, an able lawyer and a man of engaging personality and polish, who I found was an Alderman. That appeared to me at the time to be close to the Almighty in importance. I shall always remember with a great deal of gratitude the kindness of these two men to me.

That I was now engaged in the serious enterprise of life I so fully realized that I went to the barber shop and divested myself of the college fashion of long hair. Office hours were from eight to about six o'clock, during which I spent my time in reading Kent's Commentaries and in helping prepare writs, deeds, wills, and other documents.* My evenings I gave to some of the masters of English composition. I read the speeches of

---

* Coolidge's decision to read law at Hammond and Field rather than attend a formal law school shaped his conception of proper jurisprudence. Coolidge's education resembled that of a lawyer of an earlier generation, emphasizing common law. James Kent, to whom Coolidge refers, wrote and published a series of commentaries on U.S. law, relating American law to the common-law tradition of Great Britain.

Lord Erskine, of Webster, and Choate. The essays of Macaulay interested me much, and the writings of Carlyle and John Fiske I found very stimulating. Some of the orations of Cicero I translated, being especially attached to the defense of his friend the poet Archias, because in it he dwelt on the value and consolation of good literature. I read much in Milton and Shakespeare and found delight in the shorter poems of Kipling, Field and Riley.

My first Christmas was made more merry by getting notice that the Sons of the American Revolution had awarded me the prize of a gold medal worth about one hundred and fifty dollars for writing the best essay on "The Principles Fought for in the American Revolution," in a competition open to the seniors of all the colleges of the nation. The notice came one day, and it was announced in the next morning papers, where Judge Field saw it before I had a chance to tell him. So when he came to the office he asked me about it. I had not had time to send the news home. And then I had a little vanity in wishing my father to learn of it first from the press, which he did. He had questioned some whether I was really making anything of my education, in pretense I now think, not because he doubted it but because he wished to impress me with the desirability of demonstrating it.

But my main effort in those days was to learn the law. The Superior Court had three civil and two criminal terms each year in Northampton. Whenever it was sitting I spent all my time in the court room. In this way I became familiar with the practical side of trial work. I soon came to see that the counsel who knew the law were the ones who held the attention of the Judge, took the jury with them, and won their cases. They were prepared. The office where I was had a very large general practice which covered every field and took them into all the Courts of the Commonwealth but little into the Federal Courts. I assisted in the preparation of cases and went to court with the members of the firm to watch all their trial work and help keep a record of testimony for use in the arguments. It was all a work of absorbing interest to me.

The books in the office soon appeared too ponderous for my study, so I bought a supply of students' text books and law cases on the principal subjects necessary for my preparation for the bar. These enabled me to gain a more rapid acquaintance with the main legal principles, because I did not have to read through so much unimportant detail as was contained in the usual treatise prepared for a lawyer's library, which was usually a collection of all the authorities, while what I wanted was the main elements of the law. I was soon conversant with contracts, torts, evidence, and real property, with some knowledge of Massachusetts pleading, and had a considerable acquaintance with the practical side of statute law.

I do not feel that any one ever really masters the law, but it is not difficult to master the approaches to the law, so that given a certain state of facts it is possible to know how to marshal practically all the legal decisions which apply to them. I think counsel are mistaken in the facts of their case about as often as they are mistaken in the law.

All my waking hours were so fully employed that I found little time for play. My college was but eight miles distant, yet I did not have any desire to go back to the intercollegiate games, though I was accustomed to attend the alumni dinner at commencement. There was a canoe club which I joined, on the Connecticut, about a mile over the meadow from the town where I often went on Sunday afternoons. I was full of the joy of doing something in the world. Another reason why I discarded all outside enterprises and kept strictly to my work and my books was because I was keeping my monthly expenditures within thirty dollars which was furnished me by my father. He would gladly have provided me more had I needed it, but I thought that was enough and was determined to live within it, which I did. Not much was left for any unnecessary pleasantries of life.

Soon after I entered the office Mr. Hammond was elected District Attorney and Mr. Field became Mayor of the city, so that I saw something of the working of the city government and the administration of the criminal law.

The first summer I was in Northampton came the famous free silver campaign of 1896.* When Mr. Bryan was nominated he had the support of most of the local Democrats of the city, but he lost much of it before November. One of them sent a long communication to a county paper indorsing him. This I answered in one of the city papers. When I was home that summer I took part in a small neighborhood debate in which I supported the gold standard. The study I put on this subject well repaid me. Of course Northampton went handsomely for McKinley.†

With the exception of a week or two at home in the summer of 1896 I kept on in this way with my work from September, 1895, to June, 1897. I then felt sufficiently versed in the law to warrant my taking the examination for admission to the Bar. It was conducted by a County Committee of which Mr. Hammond was a member, but as I was his student he left the other two, Judge William G. Bassett and Judge William P. Strickland, to act on my petition. I was pronounced qualified by them and

---

* In the 1896 race against Republican William McKinley, Democrat William Jennings Bryan campaigned against the gold standard, calling for the unlimited coinage of silver—"free silver." Bryan gave his famous "Cross of Gold" speech at that year's Democratic National Convention.

† Northampton residents at the time overwhelmingly supported the Republican Party, as did much of New England.

just before July 4, 1897, I was duly admitted to practice before the Courts of Massachusetts. My preparation had taken about twenty months. Only after I was finally in possession of my certificate did I notify my father. He had expected that my studies would take another year, and I wanted to surprise him if I succeeded and not disappoint him if I failed. I did not fail. I was just twenty-five years old and very happy.

It was a little over eleven years from the time I left home for the Academy in the late winter of 1886 until I was admitted to the Bar in the early summer of 1897. They had been years full of experience for me, in which I had advanced from a child to a man. Wherever I went I found good people, men and women, and young folks of my own age, who had won my respect and affection. From the hearthstone of my father's fireside to the court room at Northampton they had all been kind and helpful to me. Their memory will always be one of my most cherished possessions.

My formal period of education was passed, though my studies are still pursued. I was devoted to the law, its reasonableness appealed to my mind as the best method of securing justice between man and man. I fully expected to become the kind of country lawyer I saw all about me, spending my life in the profession, with perhaps a final place on the Bench. But it was decreed to be otherwise. Some Power that I little suspected in my student days took me in charge and carried me on from the obscure neighborhood at Plymouth Notch to the occupancy of the White House.

3

THE LAW AND POLITICS

I t is one thing to know how to get admitted to the Bar but quite another thing to know how to practice law. Those who attend a law school know how to pass the examinations, while those who study in an office know how to apply their knowledge to actual practice. It seems to me that the best course is to go to a school and then go into an office where the practice is general. In that way the best preparation is secured for a thorough comprehension of the great basic principles of the profession and for their application to existing facts. Still, one who has had a good college training can do very well by starting in an office. But in any case he should not go into the law because it appears to be merely a means of making a living, but because he has a real and sincere love for the profession, which will enable him to make the sacrifices it requires.

When I decided to enter the law it was only natural, therefore, that I should consider it the highest of the professions. If I had not held that opinion it would have been a measure of intellectual dishonesty for me to take it for a life work. Others may be hampered by circumstances in making their choice, but I was free, and I went where I felt the duties would be congenial and the opportunities for service large. Those who follow other vocations ought to feel the same about them, and I hope they do.

My opinion had been formed by the high estimation in which the Bench and Bar were held by the people in my boyhood home in Vermont. It was confirmed by my more intimate intercourse with the members of the profession with whom I soon came in contact in Massachusetts after I went there to study law in the autumn of 1895. When I was admitted to practice two years later the law still occupied the high position of a profession. It had not then assumed any of its later aspects of a trade.

The ethics of the Northampton Bar were high. It was made up of men who had, and were entitled to have, the confidence and respect of their neighbors who knew them best. They put the interests of their clients above their own, and the public interests above them both. They were courteous and tolerant toward each other and respectful to the Court. This attitude was fostered by the appreciation of the uprightness and learning of the Judges.

Because of the short time I had spent in preparation I remained in the office of Hammond and Field about seven months after I was admitted to the Bar. I was looking about for a place to locate but found none that seemed better than Northampton. A new block called the Masonic Building was under construction on lower Main Street, and when it was ready for occupancy I opened an office there February 1, 1898. I had two rooms, where I was to continue to practice law for twenty-one years, until I became Governor of Massachusetts in 1919. For my office furniture and a good working library I paid about $800 from some money I had saved and inherited from my grandfather Moor. My rent was $200 per year. I began to be self-sustaining except as to the cost of my table board, which was paid by my father until September, but thereafter all my expenses I paid from the fees I received.

I was alone. While I had many acquaintances that I might call friends I had no influential supporters who were desirous to see me advanced and were sending business to me. I was dependent on the general public; what I had, came from them. My earnings for the first year were a little over $500.

My interest in public affairs had already caused me to become a member of the Republican City Committee, and in December, 1898, I was elected one of the three members of the Common Council from Ward Two. The office was without salary and not important, but the contacts were helpful. When the local military company returned that summer from the Cuban Campaign I did my best to get an armory built for them.* I was not successful at that time but my proposal was adopted a little later. This was the beginning of an interest in military preparation which I have never relinquished.

During 1899 I began to get more business. The Nonotuck Savings Bank was started early that year, and I became its counsel. Its growth was slow but steady. In later years I was its President, a purely honorary place without salary but no small honor. There was legal work about the county which came to my office, so that my fees rose to $1,400 for the second year.

I did not seek reelection to the City Council, as I knew the City Solicitor was to retire and I wanted that place. The salary was $600, which was not unimportant to me. But my whole thought was on my profession. I wanted to be City Solicitor because I believed it would make me a better lawyer. I was elected and held the office until March, 1902. It gave me a start in the law which I was ever after able to hold.

---

* The Cuban Campaign was central to the Spanish-American War of 1898.

The office was not burdensome and went along with my private practice. It took me into Court some. In a jury trial I lost two trifling cases in an action of damages against the city for taking a small strip of land to widen a highway. I felt I should have won these cases on the claim that the land in question already belonged to the highway. But I prevailed in an unimportant case in the Supreme Court against my old preceptor Mr. Hammond. It is unnecessary to say that usually my cases with him were decided in his favor. The training in this office gave me a good grasp of municipal law, that later brought some important cases to me.

In addition to the mortgage and title work of the Savings Bank, I managed some real estate, and had considerable practice in the settlement of estates. Through a collection business I also had some insolvency practice. I recall an estate in Amherst and one in Belchertown, both much involved in litigation, which I settled. In each case Stephen S. Taft of Springfield was the opposing counsel. Perhaps there is no such thing as a best lawyer, any more than there is a best book, or a best picture, but to me Mr. Taft was the best lawyer I ever saw. If he was trying a case before a jury he was always the thirteenth juryman, and if the trial was before the court he was always advising the Judge. But he did not win these cases. He became one of my best friends, and we were on the same side in several cases in later years. One time he said to me: "Young man, when you can settle a case within reason you settle it. You will not make so large a fee out of some one case in that way, but at the end of the year you will have more money and your clients will be much better satisfied." This was sound advice and I heeded it. People began to feel that they could consult me with some safety and without the danger of being involved needlessly in long and costly litigation in court. Very few of my clients ever had to pay a bill of costs. I suppose they were more reasonable than other clients, for they usually settled their differences out of court. This course did not give me much experience in the trial of cases, so I never became very proficient in that art, but it brought me a very satisfactory practice and a fair income.

I worked hard during this early period. The matters on which I was engaged were numerous but did not involve large amounts of money and the fees were small. For three years I did not take the time to visit my old home in Vermont, but when I did go I was City Solicitor. My father began to see his hopes realized and felt that his efforts to give me an education were beginning to be rewarded.

What I always felt was the greatest compliment ever paid to my professional ability came in 1903. In the late spring of that year William H. Clapp, who had been for many years the Clerk of the Courts for Hampshire County died. His ability, learning and painstaking industry made him rank very high as a lawyer. The position he held was of the first importance, for it involved keeping all the civil and criminal records of the Superior Court and the Supreme Judicial Court for the County. The Justices of the Supreme Judicial Court appointed me to fill the vacancy. I always felt this was a judgment by the highest Court in the Commonwealth on my professional qualifications. Had I been willing to accept the place permanently I should have been elected to it in the following November. The salary was then $2,300, and the position was one of great dignity, but I preferred to remain at the Bar, which might be more precarious, but also had more possibilities. Later events now known enable any one to pass judgment on my decision. Had I decided otherwise I could have had much more peace of mind in the last twenty-five years.

As the Clerk of the Courts I learned much relating to Massachusetts practice, so that ever after I knew what to do with all the documents in a trial, which would have been of much value to me if I had not been called on to give so much time to political affairs. These took up a large amount of my attention in 1904 after I went back to my office, so that my income diminished during that year. I had been chosen Chairman of the Republican City Committee. It was a time of perpetual motion in Massachusetts politics. The state elections came yearly in November, and the city elections followed in December. This was presidential year. While I elected the Representatives to the General Court by a comfortable margin at the state election I was not so successful in the city campaign. Our Mayor had served three terms, which had always been the extreme limit in Northampton, but he was nominated for a fourth time. He was defeated by about eighty votes. We made the mistake of talking too much about the deficiencies of our opponents and not enough about the merits of our own candidates. I have never again fallen into that error.* Feeling one year was all I could give to the chairmanship I did not accept a reelection but still remained on the committee.

My earnings had been such that I was able to make some small savings. My prospects appeared to be good. I had many friends and few enemies. There was a little more time for me to give to the amenities of life. I took my meals at Rahar's Inn where there was much agreeable company consisting of professional and business men of the town and some of the professors of Smith College. I had my rooms on Round Hill with the steward of the Clarke School for the Deaf. While these relations were most agreeable and entertaining I suppose I began to want a home of my own.

---

* The Republican mayor Coolidge mentions was Henry C. Hallett, who lost his bid for reelection to Democrat Theobald M. Connor in 1904. Coolidge eschewed negative campaigning throughout his career, instead finding success with voters who rewarded his civility, competence, and principled leadership.

AFTER SHE HAD FINISHED her course at the University of Vermont Miss Grace Goodhue went to the Clarke School to take the training to enable her to teach the deaf. When she had been there a year or so I met her and often took her to places of entertainment.

In 1904 Northampton celebrated its two hundred and fiftieth anniversary. One evening was devoted to a reception for the Governor and his Council, given by the Daughters of the American Revolution. Miss Goodhue accompanied me to the City Hall where the reception was held, and after strolling around for a time we sat down in two comfortable vacant chairs. Soon a charming lady approached us and said that those chairs were reserved for the Governor and Mrs. Bates and that we should have to relinquish them, which we did. Fourteen years later when we had received sufficient of the election returns to show that I had been chosen Governor of Massachusetts I turned to her and said, "The Daughters of the American Revolution cannot put us out of the Governor's chair now."

From our being together we seemed naturally to come to care for each other. We became engaged in the early summer of 1905 and were married at her home in Burlington, Vermont, on October fourth of that year. I have seen so much fiction written on this subject that I may be pardoned for relating the plain facts. We thought we were made for each other. For almost a quarter of a century she has borne with my infirmities, and I have rejoiced in her graces.

After our return from a trip to Montreal we staid a short time at the Norwood Hotel but soon started housekeeping. We rented a very comfortable house that needed but one maid to help Mrs. Coolidge do her work. Of course my expenses increased, and I had to plan very carefully for a time to live within my income. I know very well what it means to awake in the night and realize that the rent is coming due, wondering where the money is coming from with which to pay it. The only way I know of escape from that constant tragedy is to keep running expenses low enough so that something may be saved to meet the day when earnings may be small.

When the city election was approaching in December I was asked to be a candidate for School Committee. It was a purely honorary office, which had no attraction for me, but I consented and was nominated. To my surprise another Republican took out nomination papers, which split the party and elected a Democrat. The open compliment was that I had no children in the schools, but the real reason was that I was a politician. That reputation I had acquired by long service on the party committee helping elect our candidates. The man they elected gave a useful service for several years and left me free to turn to avenues which were to be much more useful to me in ways for public service. I was also better off attending to my law practice and my new home.

The days passed quietly with us until the next autumn, when we moved into the house in Massasoit Street that was to be our home for so long. I attended to the furnishing of it myself, and when it was ready Mrs. Coolidge and I walked over to it. In about two weeks our first boy came on the evening of September seventh. The fragrance of the clematis which covered the bay window filled the room like a benediction, where the mother lay with her baby. We called him John in honor of my father. It was all very wonderful to us.

We liked the house where our children came to us and the neighbors who were so kind. When we could have had a more pretentious home we still clung to it. So long as I lived there, I could be independent and serve the public without ever thinking that I could not maintain my position if I lost my office. I always made my living practicing law up to the time I became

Governor, without being dependent on any official salary. This left me free to make my own decisions in accordance with what I thought was the public good. We lived where we did that I might better serve the people.

My main thought in those days was to improve myself in my profession. I was still studying law and literature. Because I thought the experience would contribute to this end I became a candidate for the Massachusetts House of Representatives. In a campaign in which I secured a large number of Democratic votes, many of which never thereafter deserted me, I was elected by a margin of about two hundred and sixty.

The Speaker assigned me to the Committees on Constitutional Amendments and Mercantile Affairs. During the session I helped draft, and the Committee reported, a bill to prevent large concerns from selling at a lower price in one locality than they did in others, for the purpose of injuring their competitor. This seemed to me an unfair trade practice that should be abolished. We secured the passage of the bill in the House, but the Senate rewrote it in such a way that it finally failed. I also supported a resolution favoring the direct election of United States Senators and another providing for woman suffrage. These measures did not have the approbation of the conservative element of my party, but I had all the assurance of youth and ignorance in supporting them, and later I saw them all become the law.*

The next year I was reelected, but in running against a man who had a strong hold on some of the Republican Wards, my

---

* This statement hints at Coolidge's later ambivalence about progressive drives that he and his party had supported when he was a young politician. But Coolidge's support for women's suffrage remained strong throughout his life. In a 1930 newspaper column, a decade after the ratification of the Nineteenth Amendment granting women the vote, Coolidge wrote, "Nothing can be safer for the commonwealth than the informed judgment of the mothers of the land."

vote was cut down. Serving on the Judiciary Committee, which I wanted because I felt it would assist me in my profession, I became much interested in modifying the law so that an injunction could not be issued in a labor dispute to prevent one person seeking by argument to induce another to leave his employer. This bill failed. While I think it had merit, in later years I came to see that what was of real importance to the wage earners was not how they might conduct a quarrel with their employers, but how the business of the country might be so organized as to insure steady employment at a fair rate of pay. If that were done there would be no occasion for a quarrel, and if it were not done a quarrel would do no one any good.

The work in the General Court was fascinating, both from its nature and from the companionship with able and interesting men, but it took five days each week for nearly six months, so that I thought I had secured about all the benefit I could by serving two terms and declined again to be a candidate. Another boy had been given into our keeping April 13 who was named Calvin, so I had all the more reason for staying at home.

My law office took all my attention. I never had a retainer from any one, so my income always seemed precarious, but a practice which was general in its nature kept coming to me. In June of 1909 I went to Phoenix, Arizona, to hold a corporation meeting. It was the first I had seen of the West. The great possibilities of the region were apparent, and the enthusiasm of the people was inspiring. It told me that our country was sure to be a success.*

---

* Coolidge's optimism about the American West reflected his lifelong faith in the states and the concept of federalism. In a 1924 speech dedicating the Arizona State Stone in the Washington Monument, Coolidge called on America "to maintain an 'Indestructible Union of Indestructible States,'" and declared, "The Nation can be inviolate only as it insists that Arizona be inviolate."

For two years Northampton had elected a Democrat to be Mayor. He was a very substantial business man, who has since been my landlord for a long period.* He was to retire, and the Republicans were anxious to elect his successor. At a party conference it was determined to ask me to run and I accepted the opportunity, thinking the honor would be one that would please my father, advance me in my profession, and enable me to be of some public service. It was a local office, not requiring enough time to interfere seriously with my own work.

Without in any way being conscious of what I was doing I then became committed to a course that was to make me the President of the Senate of Massachusetts and of the Senate of the United States, the second officer of the Commonwealth and the country, and the chief executive of a city, a state and a nation. I did not plan for it but it came. I tried to treat people as they treated me, which was much better than my deserts, in accordance with the precept of the master poet. By my studies and my course of life I meant to be ready to take advantage of opportunities. I was ready, from the time the Justices named me the Clerk of the Courts until my party nominated me for President.

Ever I was in Amherst College I have remembered how Garman told his class in philosophy that if they would go along with events and have the courage and industry to hold to the main stream, without being washed ashore by the immaterial cross currents, they would some day be men of power. He meant that we should try to guide ourselves by general principles and not get lost in particulars. That may sound like mysticism, but it is only the mysticism that envelopes every great truth. One

* Here Coolidge refers to James W. O'Brien, who served as the Democratic mayor of Northampton from 1908 to 1910.

of the greatest mysteries in the world is the success that lies in conscientious work.

My first campaign for Mayor was very intense. My opponent was a popular merchant, a personal friend of mine who years later was to be Mayor, so that at the outset he was the favorite.* The only issue was our general qualifications to conduct the business of the city. I called on many of the voters personally, sent out many letters, spoke at many ward rallies and kept my poise. In the end most of my old Democratic friends voted for me, and I won by about one hundred and sixty-five votes.

On the first Monday of January, 1910, I began a public career that was to continue until the first Monday of March, 1929, when it was to end by my own volition.

Our city had always been fairly well governed and had no great problems. Taxes had been increasing. I was able to reduce them some and pay part of the debt, so that I left the net obligations chargeable to taxes at about $100,000. The salaries of teachers were increased. My work commended itself to the people, so that running against the same opponent for reelection my majority was much increased. I celebrated this event by taking my family to Montpelier where my father was serving in the Vermont Senate. Of all the honors that have come to me I still cherish in a very high place the confidence of my friends and neighbors in making me their Mayor.

Remaining in one office long did not appeal to me, for I was not seeking a public career. My heart was in the law. I thought a couple of terms in the Massachusetts Senate would be helpful to me, so when our Senator retired I sought his place in the fall of 1911 and was elected.

---

* Coolidge's opponent for mayor in both the 1909 and 1910 elections was Harry E. Bicknell. Bicknell would finally be elected mayor of Northampton in 1921.

The winter in Boston I did not find very satisfactory. I was lonesome. My old friends in the House were gone. The Western Massachusetts Club that had its headquarters at the Adams House, where most of us lived that came from beyond the Connecticut, was inactive. The Committees I had, except the Chairmanship of Agriculture, did not interest me greatly, and to crown my discontent a Democratic Governor sent in a veto, which the Senate sustained, to a bill authorizing the New Haven Railroad to construct a trolley system in Western Massachusetts.*

But as chairman of a special committee I had helped settle the Lawrence strike,† secured the appointment of a commission that resulted in the passage of a mothers' aid or maternity bill at the next session, and I was made chairman of a recess committee to secure better transportation for rural communities in the western part of the Commonwealth.

During the summer we did a large amount of work on that committee and made a very full and constructive report at the opening of the General Court in 1913. This was the period that the Republican party was divided between Taft and Roosevelt, so that Massachusetts easily went for Wilson.‡ But in the three-cornered contest I was reelected to the Senate.

It was in my second term in the Senate that I began to be a force in the Massachusetts Legislature. President Greenwood

---

* The "Democratic Governor" to whom Coolidge refers, here and later in this chapter, was Eugene Noble Foss, who served from 1911 to 1914.

† In 1912 textile workers in Lawrence, Massachusetts, went on strike. The "Bread and Roses" Strike, led by the Industrial Workers of the World, drew national attention and led to congressional hearings.

‡ Most of the country, in fact, easily went for Woodrow Wilson. The Democrat won 435 out of 531 electoral votes in a four-way race with the incumbent, Republican William Howard Taft; former president (and former Republican) Theodore Roosevelt, running as the Progressive (or Bull Moose) Party candidate; and socialist Eugene Debs. Coolidge's native Vermont was one of only two states Taft carried.

made me chairman of the Committee on Railroads, which I very much wanted, because of my desire better to understand business affairs, and also put me on the important Committee on Rules.* I made progress because I studied subjects sufficiently to know a little more about them than any one else on the floor. I did not often speak but talked much with the Senators personally and came in contact with many of the business men of the state. The Boston Democrats came to be my friends and were a great help to me in later times.

My committee reported a bill transforming the Railroad Commission into a Public Service Commission, with a provision intending to define and limit the borrowing powers of railroads which we passed after a long struggle and debate. The Democratic Governor vetoed the bill, but it was passed over his veto almost unanimously. The bill came out for our trolley roads in Western Massachusetts and was adopted. He vetoed this, and his veto was overridden by a large majority. It was altogether the most enjoyable session I ever spent with any legislative body.

It had been my intention to retire at the end of my second term, but the President of the Senate was reported as being a candidate for Lieutenant-Governor, and as it seemed that I could succeed him I announced that I wished for another election. When it was too late for me to withdraw gracefully President Greenwood decided to remain in the Senate. I wanted to be President of the Senate, because it was a chance to emerge from being a purely local figure to a place of state-wide distinction and authority. I knew where the votes in the Senate lay from the hard legislative contests I had conducted, and I had them fairly well organized when I found the President was not to retire.

---

* The "President Greenwood" Coolidge references is Levi H. Greenwood, president of the Massachusetts senate.

In this year of 1913 the division in the Republican party in Massachusetts was most pronounced. Our candidate for Governor fell to third place at the election, and another Democrat was made chief executive, carrying with him for the first time in a generation the whole state ticket.* But my district returned me. When I reached my office the next morning I found President Greenwood had been defeated. Again I was ready. By three o'clock that Wednesday afternoon I was in Boston, and by Monday I had enough written pledges from the Republican Senators to insure my nomination for President of the Senate at the party caucus. It had been a real contest, but all opposition subsided and I was unanimously nominated.

The Senate showed the effects of the division in our party. It had twenty-one Republicans, seventeen Democrats and two Progressives. When the vote was cast for President on the opening day of the General Court, Senator Cox the Progressive had two votes, Senator Horgan the Democrat had seven votes, and I had thirty-one votes.† I had not only become an officer of the whole Commonwealth, but I had come into possession of an influence reaching beyond the confines of my own party which I was to retain so long as I remained in public life.

Although I had arrived at the important position of President of the Massachusetts Senate in January of 1914, I had not been transported on a bed of roses. It was the result of many hard struggles in which I had made many mistakes, was to keep on making them up to the present hour, and expect to continue

---

* The Republican candidate for governor was Augustus Peabody Gardner. Democrat David I. Walsh prevailed in the election, defeating Gardner as well as Progressive Party candidate Charles Sumner Bird and incumbent Eugene Noble Foss, who broke from the Democratic Party to run as an independent.

† Coolidge defeated Charles M. Cox and Francis J. Horgan to become president of the Massachusetts senate.

to make them as long as I live. We are all fallible, but experience ought to teach us not to repeat our errors.

My progress had been slow and toilsome, with little about it that was brilliant, or spectacular, the result of persistent and painstaking work, which gave it a foundation that was solid. I trust that in making this record of my own thoughts and feeling in relation to it, which necessarily bristles with the first personal pronoun, I shall not seem to be overestimating myself, but simply relating experiences which I hope may prove to be an encouragement to others in their struggles to improve their place in the world.

It appeared to me in January, 1914, that a spirit of radicalism prevailed which unless checked was likely to prove very destructive. It had been encouraged by the opposition and by a large faction of my own party.

It consisted of the claim in general that in some way the government was to be blamed because everybody was not prosperous, because it was necessary to work for a living, and because our written constitutions, the legislatures, and the courts protected the rights of private owners especially in relation to large aggregations of property.

The previous session had been overwhelmed with a record number of bills introduced, many of them in an attempt to help the employee by impairing the property of the employer. Though anxious to improve the condition of our wage earners, I believed this doctrine would soon destroy business and deprive them of a livelihood.* What was needed was a restoration of

---

* Massachusetts Republicans and Democrats in Coolidge's day were turning toward progressivism, and Coolidge for a long time went along with them, supporting and even sponsoring progressive measures. Still, the longer he stayed in Boston, the more skeptical Coolidge became of the efficacy of progressive reform in the states. When it came to progressivism at the federal level, Coolidge mounted

confidence in our institutions and in each other, on which economic progress might rest.

In taking the chair as President of the Senate I therefore made a short address, which I had carefully prepared, appealing to the conservative spirit of the people. I argued that the government could not relieve us from toil, that large concerns are necessary for the progress in which capital and labor all have a common interest, and I defended representative government and the integrity of the courts. The address has since been known as "Have Faith in Massachusetts."* Many people in the Commonwealth had been waiting for such a word, and the effect was beyond my expectation. Confusion of thought began to disappear, and unsound legislative proposals to diminish.

The office of President of the Senate is one of great dignity and power. All the committees of the Senate are appointed by him. He has the chief place in directing legislation when the Governor is of the opposite party, as was the case in 1914. At the inauguration he presides over the joint convention of the General Court and administers the oaths of office to the Governor and Council in accordance with a formal ritual that has come from colonial days, and is much more ceremonious than the swearing-in of a President at Washington.

It did not seem to me desirable to pursue a course of partisan opposition to the Governor, and I did not do so, but rather cooperated with him in securing legislation which appeared to be for the public interest. The general lack of confidence in the country and the depression of business caused by the reduction of the tariff rates in the fall of 1913 made it necessary to grant

---

a second objection: federal progressive legislation often challenged the sovereignty of the states.

* The "Have Faith in Massachusetts" address is included in the appendix to this book.

large appropriations for the relief of unemployment during the winter. But I could see the steady decrease of the radical sentiment among the people.

In the midst of the following summer the World War enveloped Europe. It had a distinctly sobering effect upon the whole people of our country. It was very apparent in Massachusetts, where they at once began to abandon their wanderings and seek their old landmarks for guidance. The division in our party was giving way to reunion. Confidence was returning.

The Republican State Committee chose me to be chairman of the committee on resolutions at the state convention which met at Worcester, largely because of the impression made by my speech at the opening of the Senate. I drew a conservative platform, pitched in the same key, pointing out the great mass of legislation our party had placed on the statute books for the benefit of the wage earners and the welfare of the people, but declaring for the strict and unimpaired maintenance of our present social, economic and political institutions. While I did not deliver it well, in print it made an effective campaign document. After starting in the contest with little confidence, our strength increased, so that our candidate, Samuel W. McCall, received 198,627 votes and was defeated by only 11,815 plurality. All the rest of our state ticket was victorious. The political complexion of the Senate was completely changed. From a bare majority of twenty-one the Republican strength rose to thirty-three, and the opposition was reduced to seven Democrats.

My district returned me for the fourth time and I was again made President of the Senate by a unanimous vote. My opening address consisted of forty-two words, thanking the Senators for the honor and urging them in their conduct of business to be brief.

As a presiding officer it has constantly been my policy to dispatch business. It always took a long time to get all the Committees of the General Court to make their reports, but I was able to keep the daily sessions of the Senate short. I also wanted to cut down the volume of legislation. In this some progress was made. The Blue Book of Acts and Resolves for 1913 had 1,763 pages, for 1914 it had 1,423, and for 1915 only 1,230, which was a very wholesome reduction of more than thirty per cent. People were coming to see that they must depend on themselves rather than on legislation for success.

Massachusetts was beginning to suffer from a great complication of laws and restrictive regulations, from a multiplicity of Boards and Commissions, which had reached about one hundred, and from a large increase in the number of people on the public pay rolls, all of which was necessarily accompanied with a much larger cost of state government that had to be met by collecting more revenue from the taxpayers. The people began to realize that something was wrong and began to wonder whether more laws, more regulations, and more taxes, were really any benefit to them. They were becoming tired of agitation, criticism and destructive policies and wished to return to constructive methods.

When I went home at the end of the 1915 session it was with the intention of remaining in private life and giving all my attention to the law. During the winter the Lieutenant-Governor had announced that he would seek the nomination for Governor which caused some mention of me as his successor, but I was President of the Senate and did not propose to impair my usefulness in that position by involving it in an effort to secure some other office, so I gave the matter no attention. A very estimable man who had done much party service and was a brilliant platform speaker had already become a candidate, but although my record in the General Court was that of a liberal, the business interests turned to me. In this they were not alone as the event disclosed.* To the people I seemed, in some way that I cannot explain, to represent confidence. When the situation became apparent to me I went to Boston and made the simple statement in the press that I was a candidate for Lieutenant-Governor, without any reasons or any elaboration.

It was at this time that my intimate acquaintance began with Mr. Frank W. Stearns.† I had met him in a casual way for a year or two but only occasionally. In the spring he had suggested that he would like to support me for Lieutenant-Governor. He was a merchant of high character and very much respected by all who knew him, but entirely without experience in politics. He came as an entirely fresh force in public affairs, unhampered by any of the animosities that usually attach to a veteran politician. It was a great compliment to me to attract the interest of such a man, and his influence later became of large value to

---

* The lieutenant governor who sought the Republican nomination for governor was Grafton D. Cushing. As Coolidge notes later in this chapter, Samuel W. McCall ultimately received the Republican gubernatorial nomination in 1915. McCall went on to defeat the incumbent governor, Democrat David I. Walsh, who just a year earlier had won election to the office over McCall. The "very estimable man" whom Coolidge confronted in the Republican primary race for lieutenant governor was Guy Ham, a Boston lawyer known as a spellbinding orator. Coolidge won handily.

† Donors can change the course of history. That was the case with Frank Stearns, heir to the upscale Boston department store R. H. Stearns. The Stearns store, located on Tremont Street, not far from the State House, emphasized customer service over price, successfully building customer loyalty. Stearns spotted the young lawmaker from western Massachusetts early, in part because Coolidge, like himself, was a graduate of Amherst College. The initial meeting of the merchant and the senator was not a success: Stearns asked the young senator to support legislation to fund sewers in the town of Amherst. Coolidge replied that it was too late in the legislative term. The next year, however, Stearns observed that Coolidge did see the bill through—without informing Stearns. Stearns became an early Coolidge booster, supporting Coolidge's speech anthologies and convincing others of the national potential of the quiet lawmaker.

the party in the Commonwealth and nation. I always felt considerable pride of accomplishment in getting the active support of men like him. While Mr. Stearns always overestimated me, he nevertheless was a great help to me. He never obtruded or sought any favor for himself or any other person, but his whole effort was always disinterested and entirely devoted to assisting me when I indicated I wished him to do so. It is doubtful if any other public man ever had so valuable and unselfish a friend.

My activities were such that I began to see more of the Honorable W. Murray Crane.* When he came to Boston he was accustomed to have me at breakfast in his rooms at the hotel. Although he had large interests about which there was constant legislation he never mentioned the subject to me or made any suggestion about any of my official actions. Had I sought his advice he would have told me to consult my own judgment and vote for what the public interest required, without any thought of him. He confirmed my opinion as to the value of a silence which avoids creating a situation where one would otherwise not exist, and the bad taste and the danger of arousing animosities and advertising an opponent by making any attack on him. In all political affairs he had a wonderful wisdom, and in everything he was preeminently a man of judgment, who was the most disinterested public servant I ever saw and the greatest influence for good government with which I ever came in contact. What

---

* Winthrop Murray Crane (1853–1920), born into the family of the famous Massachusetts paper company, made a career at the family firm before entering politics and serving as Bay State governor and U.S. senator. Before the Seventeenth Amendment was ratified in 1913, state legislatures chose U.S. senators. Crane was a model of the pre–Seventeenth Amendment senator, devoting more time to behind-the-scenes work than to public appearances. Coolidge was not the only one to notice Crane's policy of deliberate silence. Senator Chauncey Depew of New York wrote that in the Senate, Crane "never made a speech. I do not remember that he made a motion. Yet he was the most influential member of that body."

would I not have given to have had him by my side when I was President! His end came just before the election of 1920.

These men were additional examples of good influences coming into my life, to which I referred in relating the experience of some of my younger days. I cannot see that I sought them but they came. Perhaps it was because I was ready to receive them.

In the summer of 1915 politics became very active in Massachusetts. There was a sharp campaign for the nomination for Governor, my own effort to secure the Lieutenant-Governorship, and many minor contests. I shall always remember that Augustus P. Gardner, then in Congress, honored me by becoming one of the committee of five who conducted my campaign. Many local meetings were held, calling for much speaking. In the end Samuel W. McCall was renominated for Governor. I was named as candidate for Lieutenant-Governor by a vote of about 75,000 to 50,000. The news reached my father on the one-hundredth anniversary of the birth of his father. My campaign was carried on in careful compliance with the law, and the expense was within the allowed limit of $1,500, which was contributed by numerous people. I was thus under no especial obligation to any one for raising money for me.

In the campaign for election I toured the state with Mr. McCall, making open-air speeches from automobiles during the day, and finishing with an indoor rally in the evening. It was the hardest kind of work but most fascinating. I remember that Warren G. Harding and Nicholas Longworth came into the state to promote our election and spoke with us at a large meeting one night at Lowell.*

---

* Nicholas Longworth (1869–1931), representing Ohio, served in the U.S. House of Representatives as both majority leader and Speaker of the House. Longworth played a major role in the passage of tax laws in the 1920s. He was the husband of Theodore Roosevelt's daughter Alice Roosevelt Longworth.

I did not refer to my own candidacy, but spent all my time advocating the election of Mr. McCall. He was a character that fitted into the situation most admirably. He was liberal without being visionary and conservative without being reactionary. The twenty-five years he had spent in public life gave him a remarkable equipment for discussing the issues of a campaign. Whatever information was needed concerning the state government I was in a position to supply. Much emphasis was placed by me on the urgent necessity of preventing further increases in state and national expense and of a drastic reduction wherever possible. The state was ready for that kind of a message.

When the election of 1915 came, Mr. McCall won by 6,313 votes and my plurality was 52,204. After having been held five years by Democrats, the Governorship of Massachusetts was restored to the Republican party, where it was to remain for the next fifteen years and probably much longer.* The extended struggle in which the Republicans had been engaged to restore the people of Massachusetts to their allegiance to sound government under a reunited party had at last been successful. With that prolonged effort I had been intimately associated.

The office of Lieutenant-Governor of Massachusetts differs from that of most states. As already disclosed he does not preside over the Senate. The constitution of our Commonwealth is older than the Federal Constitution and so followed the old colonial system, while most of the states have followed the Federal system. I was *ex officio* a member of the Governor's Council and chairman of the Finance and Pardon committees. As the Council met but one day each week I was pleased with the

---

* The governorship of Massachusetts reverted to the Democratic Party in 1931 upon the election of Joseph B. Ely. Later, in 1944, Ely would challenge Franklin D. Roosevelt for the Democratic nomination for president of the United States.

renewed opportunity I expected to have to practice law. But it soon developed that I must be away so much that I asked Ralph W. Hemenway to become associated with me, and he has since carried on my law office so successfully that it has become his law office rather than mine.

It has become the custom in our country to expect all Chief Executives, from the President down, to conduct activities analogous to an entertainment bureau. No occasion is too trivial for its promoters to invite them to attend and deliver an address. It appeared to be the practice of Governor McCall to accept all these invitations and when the time came, to attend what he could of them, and parcel the rest out among his subordinates. In this way I became very much engaged. It was an honor to represent the Governor, and a part of my duties according to our practice. Some days I went to several meetings for that purpose, ranging well into the night, so I was obliged to stay in Boston most of the time.

It was during this period that I wrote nearly all of the speeches afterwards published in "Have Faith in Massachusetts."* They were short and mostly committed to memory for delivery. This forced me to be a constant student of public questions.

It did not seem best for me to take a very active part in the Presidential primaries of 1916, but I quietly supported the regular ticket for delegates, which was elected. We had at least three candidates for President in Massachusetts, with all of whom I was on friendly terms, as I had never allied myself with any faction of the party, but I felt the convention did the wise thing in turning to the great statesman Charles Evans Hughes, and I supported him actively in the campaign for election. He carried

---

* Houghton Mifflin published *Have Faith in Massachusetts*, a collection of Coolidge's speeches, in 1919. The book helped Coolidge develop a national profile.

Massachusetts by a small vote. My renomination came without opposition, as did that of the Governor, who had a plurality of 46,240 at the election. My own was 84,930.

During the summer I had been chairman of a special commission to consider the financial condition of the Boston Elevated Street Railway, and helped make a report recommending that the Governor be authorized to appoint a Board of Trustees who should have the control of this property and be vested with authority to fix a rate of fare sufficient to pay the costs of operation and a fair return to the stockholders. This was adopted by the General Court and solved the pressing problem of street railway transportation, which became so acute on account of the increasing costs of operation. Later the plan was applied to the other large company in the eastern part of the state. It was not perfect, but saved the properties from destruction and gave a fair means of travel at cost, which was to be ascertained by public authority.

It was in the ensuing year that the United States entered the World War. While this took most of our thoughts off local affairs it did not prevent opposition to the renomination of Governor McCall. Had it been successful it would have deferred any chance for me to run for Governor for two or three years and probably indefinitely. Under the circumstances most of my friends supported the Governor, and he was renominated by a wide margin. I had no opposition. But interest in the election was not great, so that the vote was light. Nevertheless the Governor ran 90,479 votes ahead of his nearest competitor. In my own contest my opponent secured the Democratic, the Progressive and the Prohibition nomination. I did not think the combination would prove helpful to him, and it did not. He fell off 77,000 from the vote of his predecessor, and I won by 101,731.

While the United States had been engaged in the World War every public man, and I among them, had been constantly employed in its many activities. It increased every function of government from the administration in Washington down to the smallest town office. The whole nation seemed to be endowed with a new spirit, unified and solidified and willing to make any sacrifice for the cause of liberty. I was constantly before public gatherings explaining the needs of the time for men, money and supplies. Sometimes I was urging subscriptions for war loans, sometimes contributions to the great charities, or again speaking to the workmen engaged in construction or the manufacture of munitions. The response which the people made and the organizing power of the country were all manifestations that it was wonderful to contemplate. The entire nation awoke to a new life.

It was no secret that I desired to be Governor. Under the custom of promotion in Massachusetts a man who did not expect to be advanced would scarcely be willing to be Lieutenant-Governor. But I did nothing in the way of organizing my friends to secure the nomination. It is much better not to press a candidacy too much, but to let it develop on its own merits without artificial stimulation. If the people want a man they will nominate him, if they do not want him he had best let the nomination go to another.

The Governor very much desired to be United States Senator, but made no statement indicating he would seek that honor which would cause him to retire from his present office. Neither I nor my friends approached him or sought to influence him. Finally he called me aside and told me to announce that I would run for Governor, which I did. As no one knew what he had told me, some supposed I would run against him, which I would not have done.

I had a strong liking for this veteran public servant, and so I felt sure he liked me. He was away on many occasions, which under the constitution left me as Acting Governor, but at such times I was always careful not to encroach upon his domain. While I may have differed with my subordinates I have always supported loyally my superiors. They have never found me organizing a camp in opposition to them. Finally the Governor sought the Senatorship, but before his campaign was under way he very manfully announced that as the country was at war he was entirely unwilling to divert public attention from the national defense to promote his political fortune and therefore withdrew. My nomination was again unanimous.

The campaign was difficult. The really great qualities of my principal colleague, Senator John W. Weeks, had been displayed mostly in Washington and were not appreciated by his home people. A violent epidemic of influenza prevented us from having a State Convention, or holding the usual meetings, and the party organization was not very effective. In spite of my protest and the fact that we were engaged in a tremendous war, criticism was too often made of President Wilson and his administration. My own efforts were spent in urging that the people and government of Massachusetts should all join in their support of the national government in prosecuting the war. While I was elected by only 16,773, Senator Weeks to my lasting regret was defeated, so the state and nation lost for a time the benefit of his valuable public service. Later he was in the Cabinet where he remained until, during my term, he retired due to ill health, and did not long survive.*

Again I supposed I had reached the summit of any possible political preferment and was quite content to finish my public career as Governor of Massachusetts—an office that has

---

* John W. Weeks (1860–1926) represented Massachusetts in both the U.S. House of Representatives and the U.S. Senate. He would serve as secretary of war from 1921 until 1925. He suffered a stroke that forced him to resign.

always been held in the highest honor by the people of the Commonwealth.

To get a few days' rest I went to Maine the next Friday after the election. It was there that I was awakened in the middle of Sunday night to be told that the Armistice had been signed. I returned to Boston the following day to take part in the celebration. What the end of the four years of carnage meant those who remember it will never forget and those who do not can never be told. The universal joy, the enormous relief, found expression from all the people in a spontaneous outburst of thanksgiving.

While the war was done, its problems were to confront the state and nation for many years. I was to meet them as Governor and President. They will remain with us for two generations. Such is the curse of war.

In my inaugural address I dwelt on the need of promoting the public health, education, and the opportunity for employment at fair wages in accordance with the right of the people to be well born, well reared, well educated, well employed and well paid. I also stressed the necessity of keeping government expenses as low as possible, assisting in every possible way the reestablishing of the returning veterans, and reorganizing the numerous departments in accordance with a recent change of the constitution which limited their number to twenty.

There being no Executive Mansion the Governor has no especial social duties, so I kept my quarters at the Adams House, as I had always lived there when in Boston, where Mrs. Coolidge came sometimes; but as our boys needed her she staid for the most part in Northampton. She never had taken any part in my political life, but had given her attention to our home. It was not until we went to Washington that she came into public prominence and favor.

In February, President Wilson landed at Boston on his return from France and spoke at a large meeting, where I made a short address of welcome, pledging him my support in helping settle the remaining war problems. I then began a friendly personal relation with him and Mrs. Wilson which has always continued. Our service men were constantly returning and had to be aided in getting back into private employment.* About $20,000,000 was paid then out of the state treasury.

In the confusion attending the end of the war the work of legislation dragged on well into the summer. While I did not veto many of the bills which were passed, I did reject a measure to increase the salaries of members of the General Court from $1,000 to $1,500, but my objection was not sustained.

In the great upward movement of wages that had taken place those paid by street railways had not been proportionately increased. It is very difficult to raise fares, so sufficient money for this purpose had not been available, though some advances had been made. Because of this situation a strike occurred in mid-summer on the Boston Elevated that tied up nearly all the street transportation in the city district for three or four days. Finally I helped negotiate an agreement to send the matter to arbitration,

---

* Coolidge often commended American soldiers for their heroism and sacrifice in World War I, and on numerous occasions he made special note of the service of African Americans. Speaking at the dedication of the Tuskegee Hospital in 1923, Vice President Coolidge praised African American troops for exhibiting "a loyalty and devotion to the cause of America which was unsurpassed." Such a statement rings consistent with Coolidge's broader efforts to promote civil rights in a difficult era. In his First Annual Message to Congress, speaking about African Americans, the president declared: "Under our Constitution their rights are just as sacred as those of any other citizen. It is both a public and a private duty to protect those rights." He called on Congress to do everything in its power to stop "the hideous crime of lynching." Lynchings dropped dramatically during the Coolidge years. Coolidge supported civil rights in other ways as well, including with a federal appropriation to support the medical school at the historically black Howard University, where Coolidge later appeared to deliver a commencement address.

so that work was resumed. The men secured a very material raise in wages, which I feel later conditions fully justified.

In August I went to Vermont. On my return I found that difficulties in the Police Department of Boston were growing serious and made a statement to the reporters at the State House that I should support Commissioner Edwin U. Curtis in his decisions concerning their adjustment. I felt he was entitled to every confidence.

The trouble arose over the proposal of the policemen, who had long been permitted to maintain a local organization of their own, to form a union and affiliate with the American Federation of Labor. That was contrary to a long-established rule of the Department, which was agreed to by each member when he went on the force and had the effect of law.

When the policemen's union persisted in its course I was urged by a committee appointed by the Mayor to interfere and attempt to make Commissioner Curtis settle the dispute by arbitration. The Governor appoints the Commissioner and probably could remove him, but he has no more jurisdiction over his acts than he has over the Judges of the Courts; besides, I did not see how it was possible to arbitrate the question of the authority of the law, or of the necessity of obedience to the rules of the Department and the orders of the Commissioner. These principles were the heart of the whole controversy and the only important questions at issue. It can readily be seen how important they were and what the effect might have been if they had not been maintained. I decided to support them whatever the consequences might be. I fully expected it would result in my defeat in the coming campaign for reelection as Governor.*

---

* Politically, Coolidge's decision to back the police commissioner was a risky move. That fall, Coolidge was up for reelection. In the past, Coolidge had been

While I had no direct responsibility for the conduct of police matters in Boston, yet as the Chief Executive it was my general duty to require the laws to be enforced, so I remained in Boston and kept carefully informed of conditions. I knew I might be called on to act at any time.

On Sunday, September seventh, I went to Northampton by motor and remained overnight as I had an engagement to speak before a state convention of the American Federation of Labor at Greenfield Monday morning, which I fulfilled. I left that town at once for Boston, stopping at Fitchburg to call my office to learn if there were any new developments. I reached Boston after four o'clock that afternoon, and had a conference with some of the representatives of the city. I did not leave Boston again for a long time.

When it became perfectly apparent that the policemen's union was acting in violation of the rules of the Department the leaders were brought before the Commissioner on charges, tried and removed from office, whereat about three-quarters of the force left the Department in a body at about five o'clock on the afternoon of Tuesday, September ninth. This number was much larger than had been expected.

The Metropolitan Police of more than one hundred, and the State Police of thirty or forty men, had been kept in readiness and were at once put on duty, the Motor Corps of the State Guard was held at the armory, and that night I kept the Attorney General, the Adjutant General and my Secretary at my hotel to be ready to respond to any call for help. As everything

---

known for his ability to win the votes of newer Americans. Now he doubted whether he would be reelected. "People applaud me a great deal but I am not sure they will vote for me," he wrote in a September 26, 1919, letter to his father. "This was a service that had to be done and I have been glad to do it. The result wont [*sic*] matter to me but it will matter a great deal to the rest of America."

was quiet the Motor Corps went home. Around midnight bands of men appeared on the street, who broke many shop windows and carried away quantities of the goods which were on display. Many arrests were made, but the remaining police and their reinforcements were not sufficient to prevent the disorder. I knew nothing of this until morning.

The disorder of Tuesday night was most reprehensible, but it was only an incident. It had little relation to the real issues. I have always felt that I should have called out the State Guard as soon as the police left their posts. The Commissioner did not feel this was necessary. The Mayor, who was a man of high character, and a personal friend, but of the opposite party, had conferred with me.* He had the same authority as the Governor to call out all the Guard in the City of Boston. It would be very unusual for a Governor to act except on the request of the local authorities. No disorder existed, and it would have been rather a violent assumption that it was threatened, but it could have been made. Such action probably would have saved some property, but would have decided no issue. In fact it would have made it more difficult to maintain the position Mr. Curtis had taken, and which I was supporting, because the issue was not understood, and the disorder focused public attention on it, and showed just what it meant to have a police force that did not obey orders.

On reaching my office in the morning it was reported to me that the Mayor was calling out the State Guard of Boston to report about five o'clock that afternoon. He also requested me to furnish more troops. I supplemented his action by calling substantially the entire State Guard to report at once. They

---

* The mayor of Boston at the time was Democrat Andrew J. Peters, who had previously served in the U.S. House of Representatives.

gathered at their armories and were patrolling the streets in a few hours. When they came with their muskets in their hands with bayonets fixed there was little more trouble from disorder.

It was soon reported to me that the Mayor, acting under a special law, had taken charge of the police force of the city, and by putting a Guard officer in command had virtually displaced the Commissioner, who came to me in great distress. If he was to be superseded I thought the men that he had discharged might be taken back and the cause lost. Certainly they and the rest of the policemen's union must have rejoiced at his discomfort. Thinking I knew what to do, I consulted the law as is my custom. I found a general statute that gives the Governor authority to call on any police officer in the state to assist him. I showed this to the Attorney General and to Ex–Attorney General Herbert Parker, who was advising Mr. Curtis. They thought I was right and consulted a profound judge of law, Ex–Attorney General Albert E. Pillsbury, who confirmed their opinions. The strike occurred Tuesday night, the Guard were called Wednesday, and Thursday I issued a General Order restoring Mr. Curtis to his place as Commissioner in control of the police, and made a proclamation calling on all citizens to assist me in preserving order, and especially directing all police officers in Boston to obey the orders of Mr. Curtis.

This was the important contribution I made to the tactics of the situation, which has never been fully realized. To Mr. Curtis should go the credit for raising the issue and enforcing the principle that police should not affiliate with any outside body, whether of wage earners or of wage payers, but should remain unattached, impartial officers of the law, with sole allegiance to the public. In this I supported him.

When rumors started of a strike at the power house which furnished electricity for all Boston, a naval vessel was run up to the station with plenty of electricians on board ready to go over the side and keep the plant in operation. A wagon train of supplies, arms, and ammunition was brought in from Camp Devens and all the State Guard mobilized. A statement was made by President Wilson strongly condemning the defection of the police. Volunteer police began to come in, and over half a million dollars was raised by popular subscription to meet necessary expenses in caring for dependents of the Guard and even for helping the families of some of the police who left their posts. Later I helped these men in securing other employment, but refused to allow them again to be policemen. Public feeling became very much aroused. While offers of support came from every quarter the opposition was very active.

Soon, Samuel Gompers began to telegraph me asking the removal of Mr. Curtis and the reinstatement of the union policemen.[*] This required me to make a reply in which I stated among other things that "There is no right to strike against the public safety by any body, any time, any where."[†] This phrase caught the attention of the nation. It was beginning to be clear that if voluntary associations were to be permitted to substitute their will for the authority of public officials the end of our government was at hand. The issue was nothing less than whether the law which the people had made through their duly authorized agencies should be supreme.

This issue I took to the people in my campaign for reelec-

---

[*] Coolidge's mention of Samuel Gompers underscores the reality that the police strike in Boston did not take place in isolation. Although dramatic, the Boston police strike was but one example of labor unrest in cities across America, often coordinated or assisted by national organizations such as the American Federation of Labor, of which Gompers served as president.

[†] Coolidge slightly misquotes himself here. The telegram read, "There is no right to strike against the public safety by anybody, anywhere, any time."

tion as Governor. Though I was hampered by an attack of influenza and spoke but three or four times, I was able to make the issue plain even beyond the confines of Massachusetts. Many of the wage earners both organized and unorganized, who knew I had always treated them fairly, must have supported me, for I won by 125,101 votes. The people decided in favor of the integrity of their own government. President Wilson sent me a telegram of congratulations.

I felt at the time that the speeches I made and the statements I issued had a clearness of thought and revealed a power I had not before been able to express, which confirmed my belief that, when a duty comes to us, with it a power comes to enable us to perform it. I was not thinking so much of the Governorship, which I already had, as of the grave danger to the country if the voters did not decide correctly. My faith that the people would respond to the truth was justified.

The requirements of the situation as it developed seem clear and plain now, and easy to decide, but as they arose they were very complicated and involved in many immaterial issues. The right thing to do never requires any subterfuges, it is always simple and direct. That is the reason that intrigue usually falls of its own weight.

After the election I had the work of making the appointments in order to reduce the entire state administration to the limit of twenty Departments and a special session of the General Court to deal with some street railway problems, so I had little time to think of politics. But I soon learned that many people in the country were thinking of me.

The two years that I served as Governor were a time of transition from war to peace. New problems constantly arose, great confusion prevailed, nothing was settled and it was possible only to feel my way from day to day. But they were years

of progress if partly in a negative way. The new position of the
wage earners was perfected and solidified. A forty-eight-hour
week for women and minors was established by a bill passed
by the General Court, which I signed. The budget system went
fully into effect the first year I was Governor and helped keep
the state finances in good condition. The departments were
reorganized, and the street railways given relief. In my second year a bill was passed allowing the sale of beer with a
2.75 per cent alcoholic content, which I vetoed because I thought
it was in violation of the Constitution which I had sworn to
defend.* The veto was sustained. A constant struggle was going
on to keep the costs of living down and the rate of wages up.
A State Commission was held in office with increased powers
to resist profiteering in the necessaries of life. In the depression
of 1920 some of our banks and manufacturers found themselves
in difficulties. All of these things reached the Governor in
one form or another. But, in general, conditions were such that
the entire efforts of the people were engaged in easing themselves down. There was little opportunity to direct their attention towards constructive action. They were clearing away the
refuse from the great conflagration preparatory to rebuilding
on a grander and more pretentious scale. Nothing was natural,
everything was artificial. So much energy had to be expended
in keeping the ship of state on a straight course that there was
little left to carry it ahead. But when I finished my two terms in
January, 1921, the demobilization of the country was practically
complete, people had found themselves again, and were ready to

---

* Coolidge's position on prohibition reflected his belief in the supremacy of
the rule of law. In his First Annual Message to Congress, speaking about prohibition, President Coolidge said, "Free government has no greater menace than disre-
spect for authority and continual violation of law."

undertake the great work of reconstruction in which they have since been so successfully engaged. In that work we have seen the people of America create a new heaven and a new earth. The old things have passed away, giving place to a glory never before experienced by any people of our world.

4

IN NATIONAL POLITICS

No doubt it was the police strike of Boston that brought me into national prominence. That furnished the occasion and I took advantage of the opportunity. I was ready to meet the emergency. Just what lay behind that event I was never able to learn. Sometimes I have mistrusted that it was a design to injure me politically; if so it was only to recoil upon the perpetrators, for it increased my political power many fold. Still there was a day or two when the event hung in the balance, when the Police Commissioner of Boston, Edwin U. Curtis, was apparently cast aside discredited, and my efforts to give him any support indicated my own undoing. But I soon had him reinstated, and there was a strong expression of public opinion in our favor.

The year 1919 had not produced much on the positive side of our political life. President Wilson had returned from the peace conference at Paris determined to have the United States join the League of Nations as established in the final Treaty of Versailles. He found opposition in the Senate both within and without his own party. In attempting to gain the approval of the country he had made his trip across the continent and returned a broken man never to regain his strength. For eight years he had so dominated his party that it had not produced anyone else with a marked ability for leadership. During these months the contest was raging in the Senate over the peace treaty, but as a result it had put the leadership of our party in a negative position, which never appeals to the popular imagination, and besides in the country many Republicans favored a ratification of the treaty with adequate reservations. Many of the Senators on our side cast their vote for that proposal, which would have prevailed but for the opposition of the regular administration Democrats. In this confusion no dominant popular figure emerged in the Congress, but many ambitions became apparent.

Following my decisive victory in November there very soon came to be mention of me as a Presidential candidate. About Thanksgiving time Senator Lodge came to me and voluntarily requested that he should present my name to the national Republican convention.* He wished to go as a delegate with that understanding. Of course I told him I could not make any decision in relation to being a candidate, but I would try to arrange matters so that he could be a delegate at large. When he left for Washington he gave out an interview saying that Massachusetts should support me.

Very soon a movement of considerable dimensions started both in my home state and in other sections of the country to secure delegates who would support me. An old friend and long time Secretary of the Republican National Committee, James B. Reynolds, was placed in charge of the movement, and

* Henry Cabot Lodge (1850–1924) represented Massachusetts in the U.S. Senate for more than thirty years.

I was gaining considerable strength. Senator Crane in his own quiet but highly efficient way became very interested and let it be known that I had his support, as did Speaker Gillett, who is now our Senator, but then represented my home district in Congress.* They both went as delegates pledged to me.

Already several candidates were making a very active campaign. The two most conspicuous were Major General Leonard Wood and Governor Frank O. Lowden. Senator Hiram Johnson had considerable support, and in a more modest way Senator Warren G. Harding was in the field. In addition to these, several of the states had favorite sons. It soon began to be reported that very large sums of money were being used in the primaries.

When I came to give the matter serious attention, and comprehended more fully what would be involved in a contest of this kind, I realized that I was not in a position to become engaged in it. I was Governor of Massachusetts, and my first duty was to that office. It would not be possible for me, with the legislature in session, to be going about the country actively participating in an effort to secure delegates, and I was totally unwilling to have a large sum of money raised and spent in my behalf.

I soon became convinced also that I was in danger of creating a situation in which some people in Massachusetts could permit it to be reported in the press that they were for me when they were not at heart for me and would give me little support in the convention. It would, however, prevent their having to make a public choice as between other candidates and would help them in getting elected as delegates. There was nothing unusual in this situation. It was simply a condition that

* Frederick H. Gillett (1851–1935) served in the U.S. House of Representatives for more than thirty years, including six as Speaker of the House. He was elected to the U.S. Senate in 1924.

always has to be met in politics. Of course the strategy of the
other candidates was to prevent me from having a solid Massachusetts delegation. Moreover, I did not wish to use the office
of Governor in an attempt to prosecute a campaign for nomination for some other office. I therefore made a public statement
announcing that I was unwilling to appear as a candidate and
would not enter my name in any contest at the primaries. This
left me in a position where I ran no risk of embarrassing the
great office of Governor of Massachusetts. That was my answer
to the situation.

Nevertheless a considerable activity was kept up in my
behalf, and some money expended, mostly in circulating a book
of my speeches.* In the Massachusetts primaries six or seven
delegates were chosen who were for General Wood, and while
the rest were nominally for me several of them were really
more favorable to some other candidate, partly because they
supposed a Massachusetts man could never be nominated, and
if the choice was going outside the state, they had strong prefer-
ences as between the other possibilities.

At a state convention in South Dakota held very early to
express a preference for national candidates I had been declared
their choice for Vice-President. Some people in Oregon desired
to accord me a like honor. As I did not wish my name to appear
in any contest and did not care to be Vice-President I declined
to be considered for that office. In my native state of Vermont it

---

* The book of speeches, *Have Faith in Massachusetts*, is named for the famous
address Coolidge delivered in 1914 as the newly elected president of the Massachusetts senate. Coolidge supporter Frank Stearns was the moving force behind
the book, saying he believed distributing it would "be money well spent." *Have
Faith* was a success. Author Craig Fehrman notes that nearly 75,000 copies were
distributed in a few months. The book revealed the quality of Coolidge's thought
and action and helped to boost the Bay State governor to national prominence.

was proposed to enter my name in the primary as candidate for President, which I could not permit. Nevertheless it was written on the ballot by many of the voters at the polls.

When the Republican National Convention met at Chicago, Senator Lodge, who was elected its chairman, had indicated that he did not wish to present my name, so it was arranged that Speaker Gillett should make the nominating speech. Massachusetts had thirty-five delegates. On the first ballot I received twenty-eight of their votes and six others from scattering states, making my total thirty-four. As the balloting proceeded a considerable number of the Massachusetts delegates, feeling I had no chance, voted for other candidates, but a majority remained with me until the final ballot when all but one went elsewhere, and Senator Warren G. Harding was nominated. My friends in the convention did all they could for me, and several states were at times ready to come to me if the entire Massachusetts delegation would lead the way, but some of them refused to vote for me, so the support of other states could not be secured.

While I do not think it was so intended I have always been of the opinion that this turned out to be much the best for me. I had no national experience. What I have ever been able to do has been the result of first learning how to do it. I am not gifted with intuition. I need not only hard work but experience to be ready to solve problems. The Presidents who have gone to Washington without first having held some national office have been at great disadvantage. It takes them a long time to become acquainted with the Federal officeholders and the Federal Government. Meanwhile they have had difficulty in dealing with the situation.

The convention of 1920 was largely under the domination of a coterie of United States Senators. They maneuvered it into adopting a platform and nominating a President in ways that were not satisfactory to a majority of the delegates. When the same forces undertook for a third time to dictate the action of the convention in naming a Vice-President, the delegates broke away from them and literally stampeded to me.

Massachusetts did not present my name, because my friends knew I did not wish to be Vice-President, but Judge Wallace McCamant of Oregon placed me in nomination and was quickly seconded by North Dakota and some other states. I received about three-quarters of all the votes cast. When this honor came to me I was pleased to accept, and it was especially agreeable to be associated with Senator Harding, whom I knew well and liked.

When our campaign opened, the situation was complex. Many Republicans did not like the somewhat uncertain tone of the platform concerning the League of Nations. Though it was generally conceded that the bitter-enders had dictated the platform there were some who felt it was not explicit enough in denouncing the League with all its works and everything foreign, and a much larger body of Republicans were much disappointed that it did not declare in favor of ratifying the treaty with reservations.

The Massachusetts Republican State Convention in the fall of 1919 had adopted a plank favoring immediate ratification with suitable reservations which would safeguard American interests. While later the treaty had been rejected by the Senate it was still necessary to make a formal agreement of peace with the Central Powers, and for that purpose some treaty would be necessary. Many Republicans favored our entry into the League as a method of closing up the war period and helping stabilize world conditions. Senator Crane had taken that position in Massachusetts and repeated it again at Chicago.

Since that time the situation has changed. The war period has closed and a separate treaty has been made and ratified. The more I have seen of the conduct of our foreign relations the more I am convinced that we are better off out of the

League. Our government is not organized in a way that would enable us adequately to deal with it. Nominally our foreign affairs are in the hands of the President. Actually the Senate is always attempting to interfere, too often in a partisan way and many times in opposition to the President. Our country is not racially homogeneous. While the several nationalities represented here are loyal to the United States, yet when differences arise between European countries, each group is naturally in sympathy with the nation of its origin. Our actions in the League would constantly be embarrassed by this situation at home. The votes of our delegates there would all the time disturb our domestic tranquility here. We have come to realize this situation very completely now, but in 1920 it was not so clear.

At that time we were close to the war. Our sympathies were very much with our allies and a great body of sentiment in our country, which may be called the missionary spirit, was strongly in favor of helping Europe. To them the League meant an instrument for that end. That was a praiseworthy spirit and had to be reckoned with in dealing with the people in a political campaign. This sentiment was very marked in the East where it had a strong hold on a very substantial element of the Republican party.

While I was taking a short vacation in Vermont several thousand people came to my father's home to greet me. I spent most of my time, however, in preparing my speech of acceptance. The notification ceremonies were held on a pleasant afternoon in midsummer at Northampton in Allen Field, which was part of the college grounds, and its former President, the venerable Dr. L. Clark Seelye, presided. The chairman of the notification committee was Governor Morrow of Kentucky.* A great throng

---

* The "college grounds" were those of Smith College, where Dr. Seelye served as the first president. The committee chairman was Kentucky's Edwin P. Morrow.

representing many different states was in attendance to hear my address. I was careful to reassure those who feared we were not proposing to continue our cooperation with Europe in attempting to solve the war problems in a way that would provide for a permanent peace of the world.

Not being the head of the ticket, of course, it was not my place to raise issues or create policies, but I had the privilege of discussing those already declared in the platform or stated in the addresses of Senator Harding. This I undertook to do in a speech I made at Portland, Maine, where I again pointed out the wish of our party to have our country associated with other countries in advancing human welfare. Later in the campaign I reiterated this position at New York.

This was not intended as a subterfuge to win votes, but as a candid statement of party principles. It was later to be put into practical effect by President Harding, in the important treaty dealing with our international relations in the Pacific Ocean, in the agreement for the limitation of naval armaments, in the proposal to enter the World Court, and finally by me in the World Peace Treaty.* All that I said and more in justification of support of the Republican ticket by those interested in promoting peace, without committing our country to interfere where we had little interest, has been abundantly borne out by the events.

Shortly before election I made a tour of eight days, going

---

* At the Washington Naval Conference of 1921–22, the major powers agreed to reduce their number of warships dramatically, to respect one another's holdings in the Pacific, to consult with one another before taking action in the region during a crisis, and to affirm China's territorial integrity and the U.S. Open Door Policy with China. Both Harding and Coolidge favored U.S. involvement in the Permanent Court of International Justice, or World Court, but never secured congressional approval. The "World Peace Treaty" was the Kellogg-Briand Pact of 1928, an international agreement by which signatories promised not to resort to war to resolve conflicts.

from Philadelphia by special train west to Tennessee and Kentucky and south as far as North Carolina. We had a most encouraging reception on this trip, speaking out-of-doors, mostly from the rear platform during the day, with an indoor meeting at night. During the campaign I spoke in about a dozen states.

The country was already feeling acutely the results of deflation. Business was depressed. For months following the Armistice we had persisted in a course of much extravagance and reckless buying. Wages had been paid that were not earned. The whole country, from the national government down, had been living on borrowed money. Pay day had come, and it was found our capital had been much impaired. In an address at Philadelphia I contended that the only sure method of relieving this distress was for the country to follow the advice of Benjamin Franklin and begin to work and save. Our productive capacity is sufficient to maintain us all in a state of prosperity if we give sufficient attention to thrift and industry. Within a year the country had adopted that course, which has brought an era of great plenty.

When the election came it appeared that we had held practically the entire Republican vote and had gained enormously from all those groups who have been in this country so short a time that they still retain a marked race consciousness. Many of them had left Europe to escape from the prevailing conditions there. While they were loyal to the United States they did not wish to become involved in any old world disputes, were greatly relieved that the war was finished, and generally opposed to the League of Nations. Such a combination gave us an overwhelming victory.*

---

* In 1920 the Harding-Coolidge ticket won more than 60 percent of the popular vote and 404 of 531 electoral votes against Democrat James M. Cox and his running mate, Franklin D. Roosevelt.

After election it was necessary for me to attend a good many celebrations. My home town of Northampton had a large mass meeting at which several speeches were made. In Boston a series of dinners and lunches were given in my honor. Shortly before Christmas Mrs. Coolidge and I paid a brief visit to Mr. and Mrs. Harding at their home in Marion, Ohio. They received us in the most gracious manner. It was no secret to us why their friends had so much affection for them.

We discussed at length the plans for his administration. The members of his Cabinet were considered and he renewed the invitation to me, already publicly expressed, to sit with them.* The policies he wished to adopt for restoring the prosperity of the country by reducing taxes and revising the tariff were referred to more casually. He was sincerely devoted to the public welfare and desirous of improving the condition of the people.

When at last another Governor was inaugurated to take my place and the guns on Boston Common were giving him their first salute, Mrs. Coolidge and I were leaving for home from the North Station on the afternoon train which I had used so much before I was Governor. It had only day coaches and no parlor car, but we were accustomed to travel that way and only anxious to go home. For nine years I had been in public life in Boston.

DURING THE WINTER I made an address before the Vermont Historical Society at Montpelier and spoke later at the Town Hall in New York for a group of ladies who were restoring the birthplace of Theodore Roosevelt.

---

* President Harding's invitation to Coolidge to join Cabinet meetings was rare. In fact, Coolidge was the first vice president to attend cabinet meetings on a regular basis.

After a brief stay at Northampton, Mrs. Coolidge and I went to Atlanta where I spoke before the Southern Tariff Association. A great deal of hospitality was lavished upon us by the state officials and the people in the city. In a few days we went to Asheville, North Carolina, where we remained about two weeks. The Grove Park Inn entertained us with everything that could be wished, and the region was delightful.

When the Massachusetts electors met, Judge Henry P. Field of the firm where I read law, who had moved my admission to the Bar, now had the experience of nominating me for Vice-President. Twenty-four years had intervened between these two services which he performed for me.

The time soon came for us to go to Washington. A large crowd of our friends was at the station to bid us goodbye although the hour was very early. We went a few days before March 4 in order to have a little time to get settled. The Vice-President and Mrs. Marshall met us and gave us every attention and courtesy.* When Mr. and Mrs. Harding arrived, we went to the station to meet them and they took us back with them to the New Willard—where we too were staying—in the White House car President Wilson sent for them.

About ten-thirty the next morning a committee of the Congress came to escort us to the White House where the President and Mrs. Wilson joined us and we went to the Capitol. Soon President Wilson sent for me and said his health was such it would not be wise for him to remain for the inauguration and bade me goodbye. I never saw him again except at a distance, but he sent me a most sympathetic letter when I became President. Such was the passing of a great world figure.

---

* The "Vice-President" Coolidge refers to is Thomas Marshall of Indiana, who served two terms as vice president to President Woodrow Wilson.

As I had already taken a leading part in seven inaugurations and witnessed four others in Massachusetts, the experience was not new to me, but I was struck by the lack of order and formality that prevailed. A part of the ceremony takes place in the Senate Chamber and a part on the east portico, which destroys all semblance of unity and continuity. I was sworn in before the Senate and made a very brief address dwelling on the great value of a deliberative body as a safeguard of our liberties.

It was a clear but crisp spring day out-of-doors where the oath was administered to the President by Chief Justice White.* The inaugural address was able and well received. President Harding had an impressive delivery, which never failed to interest and hold his audience. I was to hear him many times in the next two years, but whether on formal occasions or in the freedom of Gridiron dinners, his charm and effectiveness never failed.

When the inauguration was over I realized that the same thing for which I had worked in Massachusetts had been accomplished in the nation. The radicalism which had tinged our whole political and economic life from soon after 1900 to the World War period was passed. There were still echoes of it, and some of its votaries remained, but its power was gone. The country had little interest in mere destructive criticism. It wanted the progress that alone comes from constructive policies.

It had been our intention to take a house in Washington, but we found none to our liking. They were too small or too large. It was necessary for me to live within my income, which was little more than my salary and was charged with the cost of sending my boys to school. We therefore took two bedrooms

---

* Edward Douglass White served on the U.S. Supreme Court for twenty-seven years, including a decade as chief justice. White was elevated to chief justice in 1910 on the nomination of President William Howard Taft, who himself would succeed White as chief justice in 1921.

with a dining room, and large reception room at the New Willard where we had every convenience.

It is difficult to conceive a person finding himself in a situation which calls on him to maintain a position he cannot pay for. Any other course for me would have been cut short by the barnyard philosophy of my father, who would have contemptuously referred to such action as the senseless imitation of a fowl which was attempting to light higher than it could roost. There is no dignity quite so impressive, and no independence quite so important, as living within your means. In our country a small income is usually less embarrassing than the possession of a large one.

But my experience has convinced me that an official residence with suitable maintenance should be provided for the Vice-President. Under the present system he is not lacking in dignity but he has no fixed position. The great office should have a settled and permanent habitation and a place, irrespective of the financial ability of its temporary occupant. While I was glad to be relieved of the responsibility of a public establishment, nevertheless, it is a duty the second officer of the nation should assume. It would be much more in harmony with our theory of equality if each Vice-President held the same position in the Capital City.*

Very much is said and written concerning the amount of dining out that the Vice-President does. As the President is not available for social dinners of course the next officer in rank is much sought after for such occasions. But like everything else that is sent out of Washington for public consumption the reports are exaggerated. Probably the average of these dinners

---

* Congress would not designate an official residence for the vice president until 1974. Today the official home of the vice president is on the grounds of the U.S. Naval Observatory in Washington.

during the season does not exceed three a week, and as the Senate is in session after twelve o'clock each week day, there is no opportunity for lunches or teas.

When we first went to Washington Mrs. Coolidge and I quite enjoyed the social dinners. As we were always the ranking guests we had the privilege of arriving last and leaving first, so that we were usually home by ten o'clock. It will be seen that this was far from burdensome. We found it a most enjoyable opportunity for getting acquainted and could scarcely comprehend how anyone who had the privilege of sitting at a table surrounded by representatives of the Cabinet, the Congress, the Diplomatic Corps and the Army and Navy would not find it interesting.

Presiding over the Senate was fascinating to me. That branch of the Congress has its own methods and traditions which may strike the outsider as peculiar, but more familiarity with them would disclose that they are only what long experience has demonstrated to be the best methods of conducting its business. It may seem that debate is endless, but there is scarcely a time when it is not informing, and, after all, the power to compel due consideration is the distinguishing mark of a deliberative body. If the Senate is anything it is a great deliberative body and if it is to remain a safeguard of liberty it must remain a deliberative body. I was entertained and instructed by the debates. However it may appear in the country, no one can become familiar with the inside workings of the Senate without gaining a great respect for it. The country is safe in its hands.

At first I intended to become a student of the Senate rules and I did learn much about them, but I soon found that the Senate had but one fixed rule, subject to exceptions of course, which was to the effect that the Senate would do anything it wanted to do whenever it wanted to do it. When I had learned that, I did not waste much time on the other rules, because they were so seldom applied. The assistant to the Secretary of the Senate could be relied on to keep me informed on other parliamentary questions. But the President of the Senate can and does exercise a good deal of influence over its deliberations. The Constitution gives him the power to preside, which is the power to recognize whom he will. That often means that he decides what business is to be taken up and who is to have the floor for debate at any specific time.

Nor is the impression that it is a dilatory body never arriving at decisions correct. In addition to acting on the thousands of nominations, and the numerous treaties, it passes much more legislation than the House. But it is true that unanimous consent is often required to close debate, and because of the great power each Senator is therefore permitted to exercise—which is often a veto power, making one Senator a majority of the ninety-six Senators—great care should be exercised by the states in their choice of Senators.* Nothing is more dangerous to good government than great power in improper hands. If the Senate has any weakness it is because the people have sent to that body men lacking the necessary ability and character to perform the proper functions. But this is not the fault of the Senate. It cannot choose its own members but has to work with what is sent to it. The fault lies back in the citizenship of the states. If the Senate does not function properly the blame is chiefly on them.

If the Vice-President is a man of discretion and character, so that he can be relied upon to act as a subordinate in such position, he should be invited to sit with the Cabinet, although some of the Senators, wishing to be the only advisers of the

---

* Alaska and Hawaii would not achieve statehood until decades after Coolidge penned his *Autobiography*. Thus, at the time he wrote, there were only ninety-six U.S. senators rather than the one hundred to which we are accustomed.

President, do not look on that proposal with favor. He may not help much in its deliberations, and only on rare occasions would he be a useful contact with the Congress, although his advice on the sentiment of the Senate is of much value, but he should be in the Cabinet because he might become President and ought to be informed on the policies of the administration. He will not learn of all of them. Much went on in the departments under President Harding, as it did under me, of which the Cabinet had no knowledge. But he will hear much and learn how to find out more if it ever becomes necessary. My experience in the Cabinet was of supreme value to me when I became President.

It was my intention when I became Vice-President to remain in Washington, avoid speaking and attend to the work of my office. But the pressure to speak is constant and intolerable. However, I resisted most of it. I was honored by the President by his request to make the dedicatory address at the unveiling of a bust of him in the McKinley Memorial at Niles, Ohio. I also delivered the address at the dedication of the Grant statue in Washington.

During these two years I spoke some and lectured some. This took me about the country in travels that reached from Maine to California, from the Twin Cities to Charleston. I was getting acquainted. Aside from speeches I did little writing, but I read a great deal and listened much. While I little realized it at the time it was for me a period of most important preparation. It enabled me to be ready in August, 1923.

An extra session of the Congress began in April of 1921, which was almost continuous until March 4, 1923. While an enormous amount of work was done it soon became apparent that the country expected too much from the change in administration. The government could and did stop the waste of the people's savings, but it could not restore them. That had to be done by the hard work and thrift of the people themselves. This would take time.

While the country was improving it was still depressed. There was some unemployment and a good deal of distress in agriculture because of the very low prices of farm produce and the shrinkage in land values. When I began to make political speeches in the campaign of 1922 I soon realized that the country had large sections that were disappointed because a return of prosperity had not been instantaneous.* Moreover the people had little knowledge of the great mass of legislation already accomplished, which was to prove so beneficial to them within a few months in the future. After I had related some of the record of the relief measures adopted they would come to me to say they had never heard of it and thought nothing had been done. While my party still held both the House and Senate it lost many seats in the election, which made the closing session of Congress full of complaints tinged with bitterness against an administration under which many of them had been defeated. That being the natural reaction it is useless to discuss its propriety.

While these years in Washington had been full of interest they were not without some difficulties. Its official circles never accept any one gladly. There is always a certain unexpressed sentiment that a new arrival is appropriating the power that

---

* Americans today are largely unaware of the severe economic recession that took place in 1920–21. Unemployment, as then measured, jumped to approximately 12 percent. President Wilson and then President Harding cut government spending rather than engage in deficit spending. By 1922, as Coolidge notes, the economy had improved significantly, though industries such as agriculture faced challenges throughout the 1920s. For more on this "forgotten depression" of the early 1920s, see *The Forgotten Depression: 1921: The Crash That Cured Itself*, by James Grant (New York: Simon & Schuster, 2014).

should rightfully belong to them. He is always regarded as in the nature of a usurper. But I think I met less of this sentiment than is usual, for I was careful not to be obtrusive. Nevertheless I could not escape being looked on as one who might be given something that others wished to have. But as it soon became apparent that I was wholly engaged in promoting the work of the Senate and the success of the administration, rather than my own interests, I was more cordially accepted.

In these two years I witnessed the gigantic task of demobilizing a war government and restoring it to a peace-time basis. I also came in contact with many of the important people of the United States and foreign countries. All talent eventually arrives at Washington. Most of the world figures were there at the Conference on Limitation of Armaments.* Other meetings brought people only a little less distinguished. While I had little official connection with these events the delegates called on me and I often met them on social occasions.

The efforts of President Harding to restore the country became familiar to me. I saw the steady increase of the wise leadership of Mr. Hughes and Mr. Mellon in the administration of the government and the passing of some of the veteran figures of the Senate.† Chief among these was Senator Knox of Pennsylvania.‡ He was a great power and had a control of the

---

* The Washington Naval Conference of 1921–22.

† Secretary of State Charles Evans Hughes and Treasury Secretary Andrew Mellon. When President Harding passed away, Coolidge ensured that Mellon stayed on at Treasury. Americans regarded Mellon so highly that later it was said that "three presidents served under him." Coolidge, who prized the principle of delegation, understood the value of continuity and talent. Mellon advised that cutting the high taxes of the Wilson administration would spur economic growth.

‡ Philander C. Knox represented Pennsylvania in the U.S. Senate and had served in the cabinets of three presidents—William McKinley, Theodore Roosevelt, and William Howard Taft. Knox died in October 1921 at the age of sixty-eight.

conduct of the business of the Senate, which he exercised in behalf of our party policies, that no one else approached during my service in Washington.

In the winter of 1923 President Harding was far from well. At his request I took his place in delivering the address at the Budget Meeting. While he was out again in a few days he never recovered. As Mrs. Coolidge and I were leaving for the long recess on the fourth of March I bade him goodbye. We went to Virginia Hot Springs for a few days and then returned to Massachusetts, where we remained while I filled some speaking engagements, and in July went to Vermont. We left the President and Mrs. Harding in Washington. I do not know what had impaired his health.* I do know that the weight of the Presidency is very heavy. Later it was disclosed that he had discovered that some whom he had trusted had betrayed him and he had been forced to call them to account. It is known that this discovery was a very heavy grief to him, perhaps more than he could bear.† I never saw him again. In June he started for Alaska and—eternity.

---

* President Warren G. Harding died August 2, 1923, at the Palace Hotel in San Francisco, where he had stopped en route back to Washington from Alaska. Although reports at the time suggested perhaps a stroke was to blame, historians now attribute the cause of death to a heart attack. Harding was fifty-seven years old.

† Here Coolidge refers, obliquely, to corruption scandals that plagued the Harding administration. Harding had appointed a close friend, Charles Forbes, director of the newly created Veterans' Bureau. In early 1923 the president confronted Forbes when he learned that his old friend had disobeyed a direct order to stop illegally selling the bureau's hospital supplies. Forbes had lined his own pockets through the sales and other corrupt schemes. In 1926 he would be convicted of conspiracy to defraud the U.S. government. The infamous Teapot Dome scandal, news of which went public only after Harding's death, centered on Secretary of the Interior Albert Fall, one of Harding's former fellow senators (and poker buddies). Fall would be convicted of taking bribes to grant oil companies exclusive leases to drill on federal land.

5

ON ENTERING
AND LEAVING THE
PRESIDENCY

I t is a very old saying that you never can tell what you can do until you try. The more I see of life the more I am convinced of the wisdom of that observation.

Surprisingly few men are lacking in capacity, but they fail because they are lacking in application. Either they never learn how to work, or, having learned, they are too indolent to apply themselves with the seriousness and the attention that is necessary to solve important problems.

Any reward that is worth having only comes to the industrious. The success which is made in any walk of life is measured almost exactly by the amount of hard work that is put into it.

It has undoubtedly been the lot of every native boy of the United States to be told that he will some day be President. Nearly every young man who happens to be elected a member of his state legislature is pointed to by his friends and his local newspaper as on the way to the White House.

My own experience in this respect did not differ from that of others. But I never took such suggestions seriously, as I was convinced in my own mind that I was not qualified to fill the exalted office of President.

I had not changed this opinion after the November elections of 1919, when I was chosen Governor of Massachusetts for a second term by a majority which had only been exceeded in 1896.

When I began to be seriously mentioned by some of my friends at that time as the Republican candidate for President, it became apparent that there were many others who shared the same opinion as to my fitness which I had so long entertained.

But the coming national convention, acting in accordance with an unchangeable determination, took my destiny into its own hands and nominated me for Vice-President.

Had I been chosen for the first place, I could have accepted it only with a great deal of trepidation, but when the events of August, 1923, bestowed upon me the Presidential office, I felt at once that power had been given me to administer it.* This was not any feeling of exclusiveness. While I felt qualified to serve, I was also well aware that there were many others who were better qualified. It would be my province to get the benefit of their opinions and advice. It is a great advantage to a President, and a major source of safety to the country, for him to know that he is not a great man. When a man begins to feel that he is the only one who can lead in this republic, he is guilty of treason to the spirit of our institutions.

After President Harding was seriously stricken, although I noticed that some of the newspapers at once sent representatives to be near me at the home of my father in Plymouth, Vermont, the official reports which I received from his bedside soon became so reassuring that I believed all danger past.

* Shortly after becoming president, Coolidge remarked, "I believe I can swing it."

On the night of August 2, 1923, I was awakened by my father coming up the stairs calling my name. I noticed that his voice trembled. As the only times I had ever observed that before were when death had visited our family, I knew that something of the gravest nature had occurred.

His emotion was partly due to the knowledge that a man whom he had met and liked was gone, partly to the feeling that must possess all of our citizens when the life of their President is taken from them.

But he must have been moved also by the thought of the many sacrifices he had made to place me where I was, the twenty-five-mile drives in storms and in zero weather over our mountain roads to carry me to the academy and all the tenderness and care he had lavished upon me in the thirty-eight years since the death of my mother in the hope that I might sometime rise to a position of importance, which he now saw realized.

He had been the first to address me as President of the United States. It was the culmination of the lifelong desire of a father for the success of his son.

He placed in my hands an official report and told me that President Harding had just passed away. My wife and I at once dressed.

Before leaving the room I knelt down and, with the same prayer with which I have since approached the altar of the church, asked God to bless the American people and give me power to serve them.

My first thought was to express my sympathy for those who had been bereaved and after that was done to attempt to reassure the country with the knowledge that I proposed no sweeping displacement of the men then in office and that there were to be no violent changes in the administration of affairs.

As soon as I had dispatched a telegram to Mrs. Harding, I therefore issued a short public statement declaratory of that purpose.

Meantime, I had been examining the Constitution to determine what might be necessary for qualifying by taking the oath of office. It is not clear that any additional oath is required beyond what is taken by the Vice-President when he is sworn into office. It is the same form as that taken by the President.

Having found this form in the Constitution I had it set up on the typewriter and the oath was administered by my father in his capacity as a notary public, an office he had held for a great many years.

The oath was taken in what we always called the sitting room by the light of the kerosene lamp, which was the most modern form of lighting that had then reached the neighborhood. The Bible which had belonged to my mother lay on the table at my hand. It was not officially used, as it is not the practice in Vermont or Massachusetts to use a Bible in connection with the administration of an oath.

Besides my father and myself, there were present my wife, Senator Dale, who happened to be stopping a few miles away, my stenographer, and my chauffeur.*

The picture of this scene has been painted with historical accuracy by an artist named Keller, who went to Plymouth for that purpose.† Although the likenesses are not good, everything in relation to the painting is correct.

---

* At the time of Coolidge's inauguration, Porter H. Dale (1867–1933) represented Vermont in the U.S. House of Representatives. Dale happened to be campaigning in the area. That November he would be elected to the U.S. Senate to complete the term of William P. Dillingham, who had died in July. Erwin C. Geisser was Coolidge's stenographer. The president's chauffeur was Joseph M. McInerney.

† The artist was Arthur J. Keller. The painting is reproduced in the photo section of this book.

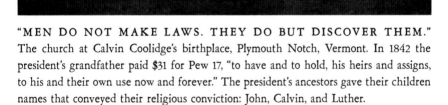

"MEN DO NOT MAKE LAWS. THEY DO BUT DISCOVER THEM."
The church at Calvin Coolidge's birthplace, Plymouth Notch, Vermont. In 1842 the president's grandfather paid $31 for Pew 17, "to have and to hold, his heirs and assigns, to his and their own use now and forever." The president's ancestors gave their children names that conveyed their religious conviction: John, Calvin, and Luther.

"THEY WERE A HARDY, SELF-CONTAINED PEOPLE." The still-isolated hamlet of Plymouth Notch in the late 1800s. Locals relished the independence of rural life but grew frustrated when that great connector of the 1800s, the railroad, passed Plymouth by.

BORN ON THE FOURTH OF JULY. John and Victoria Coolidge's son, John Calvin Coolidge, was born on July 4, 1872, making Coolidge the only president to share a birthday with the nation. A sister, Abigail Gratia Coolidge, arrived three years later. When Coolidge was twelve, his mother passed away. For high school, Coolidge's father sent the boy ten miles away, to Ludlow, Vermont.

"INTO THE LIGHT." Calvin welcomed the chance to enter the larger world of the railway town of Ludlow. The Black River Academy pupil liked learning Latin—algebra, less so. With his sister, Abbie, Coolidge operated a debate club. In the big world of Ludlow, he also came to understand the importance of dress and demeanor. "Would you be willing that I should get a suit of clothes this spring?" Coolidge wrote his father from high school. "Moore has something that suits me … price about 17 dollars. I know my expenses are very large." Coolidge's father did supply clothes, including some items when his son went off to college at Amherst in Massachusetts (*right*).

"IF I HAD LET MY FAILURES..." Coolidge's start at Amherst College proved difficult, in part perhaps because his sister had recently passed away. By senior year, however, the undergraduate surprised others by finding his voice through the sport of debate. It was as though "a new and gifted man" had joined the class, a class-mate commented. *Above:* An Amherst library.

READING LAW. Instead of enrolling in law school after college, as fellow Amherst alumni Harlan Stone and Dwight Morrow did, Coolidge chose the practical course of "reading law." Coolidge clerked at Hammond and Field, a law firm in Northampton, Massachusetts. *Right:* The young attorney strides the streets of Northampton.

"I HAVE REJOICED IN HER GRACES." Coolidge entered politics early, rising from city councilman to state representative to Northampton mayor to state senator. In 1905 the bachelor's life transformed when he married Grace Anna Goodhue (*left*), a graduate of a teaching program at the Clarke School for the Deaf. Grace's mother had suggested the pair wait a year before marrying while Grace learned to bake bread and keep house. "We can buy bread," Coolidge snapped, and the wedding took place without delay. Sons John (born 1906) and Calvin Jr. (1908) completed the family.

"HAVE FAITH IN MASSACHUSETTS." By the time Coolidge became Massachusetts governor (*above*), he had more than twenty years' experience in politics under his belt. The young lawmaker at first backed progressive legislation. Over time, however, Coolidge came to question the rapid reform progressives advocated. "It is much more important to kill bad bills than to pass good ones," he counseled his father in 1910.

CRUCIAL MENTORS. Department store executive Frank Stearns supported Coolidge publicly as the politician climbed in Massachusetts. Coolidge's political mentor was the U.S. senator Winthrop Murray Crane (*left*), of the paper company family. Crane's silent—and successful—style made an impression on Coolidge, who preferred Crane to another Bay State senator, Henry Cabot Lodge.

NORMALCY. The U.S. had prevailed in World War I, but it was not clear America would win the peace. Coolidge friend Dwight Morrow pushed hard for Coolidge at the 1920 Republican National Convention, but Warren Harding *(left, with Coolidge)* won the presidential nomination, and Coolidge the second spot. The Harding-Coolidge agenda called for "normalcy"—stable conditions that would enable America to move forward, including lower taxes, less regulation, and the rule of law. Americans voted them in.

INAUGURATION BY KEROSENE LIGHT. Harding's political scandals began to cast a shadow over his administration. One summer night in August 1923, news of Harding's death reached the Coolidges at Plymouth Notch. By virtue of his authority as a notary, Coolidge's father swore the son into office. Artists later captured the historic scene.

"HAVE FAITH IN MASSACHUSETTS." By the time Coolidge became Massachusetts governor (*above*), he had more than twenty years' experience in politics under his belt. The young lawmaker at first backed progressive legislation. Over time, however, Coolidge came to question the rapid reform progressives advocated. "It is much more important to kill bad bills than to pass good ones," he counseled his father in 1910.

CRUCIAL MENTORS. Department store executive Frank Stearns supported Coolidge publicly as the politician climbed in Massachusetts. Coolidge's political mentor was the U.S. senator Winthrop Murray Crane (*left*), of the paper company family. Crane's silent—and successful—style made an impression on Coolidge, who preferred Crane to another Bay State senator, Henry Cabot Lodge.

"THERE IS NO RIGHT TO STRIKE." War's end abroad did not bring peace at home. When in 1919 the Boston police force broke its contract and walked out on strike, mayhem ensued (*above*). Governor Coolidge risked losing that autumn's election when he backed the police commissioner's controversial decision to fire the policemen. *Below:* Governor Coolidge poses resolutely in a police vehicle. "There is no right to strike against the public safety by anybody, anywhere, any time," Coolidge wrote.

INTO THE SPOTLIGHT. Sudden prominence for a politician means new responsibility for his family as well. *Above:* Coolidge poses with his sons at the family home in Northampton. Elder son John wears the flag. Years later, when Calvin Jr. worked in a tobacco field (*below, right*), a fellow worker told him he wouldn't do such work if his father were president. "If my father were your father, you would," Calvin replied.

NORMALCY. The U.S. had prevailed in World War I, but it was not clear America would win the peace. Coolidge friend Dwight Morrow pushed hard for Coolidge at the 1920 Republican National Convention, but Warren Harding (*left, with Coolidge*) won the presidential nomination, and Coolidge the second spot. The Harding-Coolidge agenda called for "normalcy"—stable conditions that would enable America to move forward, including lower taxes, less regulation, and the rule of law. Americans voted them in.

INAUGURATION BY KEROSENE LIGHT. Harding's political scandals began to cast a shadow over his administration. One summer night in August 1923, news of Harding's death reached the Coolidges at Plymouth Notch. By virtue of his authority as a notary, Coolidge's father swore the son into office. Artists later captured the historic scene.

"I BELIEVE I CAN SWING IT." Moved as he was at Harding's passing, Coolidge affirmed that he would strive to meet the goals the Republican Party had established in 1920. The accidental president quickly won the confidence of the country. He found a powerful partner in Treasury Secretary Andrew Mellon (*below, center, with Coolidge and Herbert Hoover*), who put forward dramatic tax-reduction plans. Coolidge focused his energies on budgeting and cutting taxes. When the White House received twin lion cubs as a gift, the president named them "Budget Bureau" and "Tax Reduction."

AN AWFUL VIGIL. During the 1924 campaign, tragedy struck: the Coolidges' sixteen-year-old son, Calvin Jr., fell ill when a blister he sustained playing tennis led to blood poisoning. *Above:* Americans keep vigil outside the White House as the boy sickens. After Calvin Jr.'s death, the president struggled—and persevered. *Below:* At his father's home in Plymouth Notch, the mourning chief executive and first lady receive key innovators of the era—Harvey Firestone, Henry Ford, and Thomas Edison.

"IF ALL MEN ARE CREATED EQUAL, THAT IS FINAL."

The country overwhelmingly supported immigration restriction, and Coolidge signed the restrictive Immigration Act of 1924. But the president went out of his way to demonstrate deep appreciation for the contributions and sacrifices of Americans at home. Coolidge explicitly defended the rights of African Americans to run for office—rights that others challenged. He was the first president to seat a woman on the federal bench. He signed a law ensuring Native Americans citizenship. *Right:* The president poses with Thomas Lee, who saved thirty-two people from a sinking boat on the Mississippi River. Although Coolidge vetoed benefits for veterans, he appreciated their service and supported their care. *Below:* President and Mrs. Coolidge greet veterans.

AN EARNED VICTORY. Americans liked Coolidge's respect for business, big and small, as well as his careful budgeting. They also appreciated his respect for traditions, both old and new. *Above:* Citizens greet Coolidge at John Adams's home in Quincy, Massachusetts. *Below:* Coolidge throws out the first pitch at a 1924 World Series game. A month later, Americans returned Coolidge to office; he took more votes than the candidates of the two other parties, the Democrats and the Progressives, combined.

CONNECTING AMERICA, AND THE WORLD. One reason social tensions eased in the later 1920s was that life improved. In the 1920s new technology gave families their first car, their first radio, indoor plumbing, electricity, vacations, and Saturday off—the last a gift of increased productivity. *Above:* Coolidge inspects new autos. Coolidge believed in technology's power to connect not only the nation but the world as well. *Below:* Coolidge becomes the first president to hold a transatlantic telephone call, with Spain's King Alfonso.

THAT TWENTIES ROAR.
Coolidge policies gave America the Roaring Twenties, which helped ensure U.S. economic primacy across the globe, a fact that pleased him deeply. The lighter side of the Roaring Twenties also delighted Coolidge. *Left:* He and Mrs. Coolidge test equipment for a new form of tourism, the ski vacation. Perhaps the memory of the challenges of isolated Plymouth fostered the Coolidge interest. *Below:* The president's father tries out a winter stagecoach on blades.

TESTED BY TWO FLOODS. When the Great Mississippi River Flood devastated the South, Coolidge chose not to travel there, in part because he believed state governments should lead disaster recovery. Observers commented acidly that Coolidge would react differently if a flood destroyed his own New England. That year a flood indeed laid waste to Vermont (*above*). Coolidge chose not to travel there either. "He can't do for his own, you see, more than he did for the others," said one New Englander, a sentiment many citizens shared. *Below:* Vermonters welcome Coolidge a year after the flood.

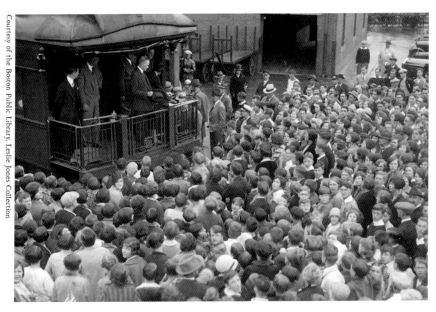

"RETURN TO THE PEOPLE." The Republican Party was eager for the popular president to run again in 1928. But like George Washington before him, Coolidge believed presidents shouldn't serve too long, and in 1929 he rode back to Northampton with Grace (*above*). In January 1933, Coolidge passed away at the age of sixty. He was buried in Vermont beside his family at Plymouth Notch (*below*). "In due time," wrote the *Wall Street Journal*'s editors, "the good fortune of the United States to have had such a man as Calvin Coolidge in just the years he filled that office will be more clearly realized than it has yet been."

Where succession to the highest office in the land is by inheritance or appointment, no doubt there have been kings who have participated in the induction of their sons into their office, but in republics where the succession comes by an election I do not know of any other case in history where a father has administered to his son the qualifying oath of office which made him the chief magistrate of a nation. It seemed a simple and natural thing to do at the time, but I can now realize something of the dramatic force of the event.

This room was one which was already filled with sacred memories for me. In it my sister and my stepmother passed their last hours. It was associated with my boyhood recollections of my own mother, who sat and reclined there during her long invalid years, though she passed away in an adjoining room where my father was to follow her within three years from this eventful night.

When I started for Washington that morning I turned aside from the main road to make a short devotional visit to the grave of my mother. It had been a comfort to me during my boyhood when I was troubled to be near her last resting place, even in the dead of night. Some way, that morning, she seemed very near to me.

A telegram was sent to my pastor, Dr. Jason Noble Pierce, to meet me on my arrival at Washington that evening, which he did.

I found the Cabinet mostly scattered. Some members had been with the late President and some were in Europe. The Secretary of State, Mr. Hughes, and myself, at once began the preparation of plans for the funeral.

I issued the usual proclamation.

The Washington services were held in the rotunda of the Capitol, followed by a simple service and interment at Marion, Ohio, which I attended with the Cabinet and a large number of officers of the government.

The nation was grief-stricken. Especially noticeable was the deep sympathy every one felt for Mrs. Harding. Through all this distressing period her bearing won universal commendation. Her attitude of sympathy and affection towards Mrs. Coolidge and myself was an especial consolation to us.

The first Sunday after reaching Washington we attended services, as we were accustomed to do, at the First Congregational Church. Although I had been rather constant in my attendance, I had never joined the church.*

While there had been religious services, there was no organized church society near my boyhood home. Among other things, I had some fear as to my ability to set that example which I always felt ought to denote the life of a church member. I am inclined to think now that this was a counsel of darkness.

This first service happened to come on communion day. Our pastor, Dr. Pierce, occupied the pulpit, and, as he can under the practice of the Congregational Church, and always does, because of his own very tolerant attitude, he invited all those who believed in the Christian faith, whether church members or not, to join in partaking of the communion.

For the first time I accepted this invitation, which I later learned he had observed, and in a few days without any intimation to me that it was to be done, considering this to be a sufficient public profession of my faith, the church voted me into its membership.

This declaration of their belief in me was a great satisfaction.

Had I been approached in the usual way to join the church

---

* Grace Coolidge took the lead when it came to the Coolidge family's religious observance. Though raised a Methodist, as a teen Grace joined the College Street Congregational Church and sang in the choir. In Northampton, the Coolidge family attended the storied Edwards Church, founded in the name of the theologian Jonathan Edwards in 1833.

after I became President, I should have feared that such action might appear to be a pose, and should have hesitated to accept. From what might have been a misguided conception I was thus saved by some influence which I had not anticipated.

But if I had not voluntarily gone to church and partaken of communion, this blessing would not have come to me.

Fate bestows its rewards on those who put themselves in the proper attitude to receive them.

During my service in Washington I had seen a large amount of government business. Peace had been made with the Central Powers, the tariff revised, the budget system adopted, taxation reduced, large payments made on the national debt, the Veterans' Bureau organized, important farm legislation passed, public expenditures greatly decreased, the differences with Colombia of twenty years' standing composed, and the Washington Conference had reached an epoch-making agreement for the practical limitation of naval armaments.

It would be difficult to find two years of peacetime history in all the record of our republic that were marked with more important and far-reaching accomplishments. From my position as President of the Senate, and in my attendance upon the sessions of the Cabinet, I thus came into possession of a very wide knowledge of the details of the government.

In spite of the remarkable record which had already been made, much remained to be done. While anything that relates to the functions of the government is of enormous interest to me, its economic relations have always had a peculiar fascination for me.

Though these are necessarily predicated on order and peace, yet our people are so thoroughly law-abiding and our foreign relations are so happy that the problem of government action which is to carry its benefits into the homes of all the people becomes almost entirely confined to the realm of economics.

My personal experience with business had been such as comes to a country lawyer.

My official experience with government business had been of a wide range. As Mayor, I had charge of the financial affairs of the City of Northampton. As Lieutenant-Governor, I was Chairman of the Committee on Finance of the Governor's Council, which had to authorize every cent of the expenditures of the Commonwealth before they could be made. As Governor, I was chargeable with responsibility both for appropriations and for expenditures.

My fundamental idea of both private and public business came first from my father. He had the strong New England trait of great repugnance at seeing anything wasted. He was a generous and charitable man, but he regarded waste as a moral wrong.

Wealth comes from industry and from the hard experience of human toil. To dissipate it in waste and extravagance is disloyalty to humanity. This is by no means a doctrine of parsimony. Both men and nations should live in accordance with their means and devote their substance not only to productive industry, but to the creation of the various forms of beauty and the pursuit of culture which give adornments to the art of life.

When I became President it was perfectly apparent that the key by which the way could be opened to national progress was constructive economy. Only by the use of that policy could the high rates of taxation, which were retarding our development and prosperity, be diminished, and the enormous burden of our public debt be reduced.*

---

* By the time Coolidge took office, the top tax rate on individual income was well below the World War I high of 77 percent. Coolidge, determined to cut further, managed to bring the top rate down to 25 percent. Coolidge, however, never called for tax cuts without seeking matching budget cuts. In public, the president took every chance to pair the two explicitly—even when it came to naming his

Without impairing the efficient operation of all the functions of the government, I have steadily and without ceasing pressed on in that direction. This policy has encouraged enterprise, made possible the highest rate of wages which has ever existed, returned large profits, brought to the homes of the people the greatest economic benefits they ever enjoyed, and given to the country as a whole an unexampled era of prosperity. This well-being of my country has given me the chief satisfaction of my administration.*

One of my most pleasant memories will be the friendly relations which I have always had with the representatives of the press in Washington. I shall always remember that at the conclusion of the first regular conference I held with them at the White House office they broke into hearty applause.

I suppose that in answering their questions I had been fortunate enough to tell them what they wanted to know in such a way that they could make use of it.

While there have been newspapers which supported me, of course there have been others which opposed me, but they have

---

pets. When the Coolidges received the gift of twin lion cubs, he named them "Budget Bureau" and "Tax Reduction." The outcome of Coolidge fiscal policies were as he hoped. When Coolidge left office, federal outlays were lower than they had been when he had taken office sixty-seven months earlier. By the time Coolidge left office, the federal debt had dropped by nearly one-third from its postwar high. Though the Coolidge administration and Congress had cut tax rates, increased business activity guaranteed that a healthy share of tax revenue still flowed to Washington. The wealthy paid a greater share of federal taxes than they had before the Harding-Coolidge tax cuts.

* The evidence suggests that the country benefited mightily from Coolidge policy. Economic growth proved strong in the 1920s, with relatively low unemployment. What stands out especially is the improvement in the quality of life. At the beginning of the decade, indoor plumbing was more an exception than the rule. By the end, the majority of households had toilets. Electrification and the rise of the radio and telephone improved life at work and at home. Productivity gains meant many workers could give up the traditional six-day-a-week grind and still make a good living. The 1920s gave America the gift of Saturday off.

usually been fair. I shall always consider it the highest tribute to my administration that the opposition have based so little of their criticism on what I have really said and done.

I have often said that there was no cause for feeling disturbed at being misrepresented in the press.* It would be only when they began to say things detrimental to me which were true that I should feel alarm.

Perhaps one of the reasons I have been a target for so little abuse is because I have tried to refrain from abusing other people.

The words of the President have an enormous weight and ought not to be used indiscriminately.

It would be exceedingly easy to set the country all by the ears and foment hatreds and jealousies, which, by destroying faith and confidence, would help nobody and harm everybody. The end would be the destruction of all progress.

While every one knows that evil exists, there is yet sufficient good in the people to supply material for most of the comment that needs to be made.

The only way I know to drive out evil from the country is by the constructive method of filling it with good. The country is better off tranquilly considering its blessings and merits, and earnestly striving to secure more of them, than it would be in nursing hostile bitterness about its deficiencies and faults.

---

* In Coolidge's era, it was generally expected that the press would criticize those in public life. Coolidge took his share of abuse—the journalistic legend H. L. Mencken said Coolidge was "as appalling and as fascinating as a two-headed boy." Yet Coolidge managed to ignore critics whose charges seemed to him unfounded, and he maintained a professional and largely positive relationship with the media. Coolidge averaged nearly two press conferences per week. At that time reporters submitted questions in advance and were permitted to use the president's responses only as background for their stories. Transcripts of Coolidge's press conferences show the president chiding reporters when they violated this agreement, warning he would not be so candid in his responses should they not respect the rules.

Notwithstanding the broad general knowledge which I had of the government, when I reached Washington I found it necessary to make an extensive survey of the various Departments to acquaint myself with details. This work had to be done intensively from the first of August to the middle of November, in order to have the background and knowledge which would enable me to discuss the state of the Union in my first Message to the Congress.

Although meantime I was pressed with invitations to make speeches, I did not accept any of them. The country was in mourning and I felt it more appropriate to make my first declaration in my Message to the Congress. Of course, I opened the Red Cross Convention in October, which was an official function for me as its President.

I was especially fortunate in securing C. Bascom Slemp as my Secretary, who had been a member of the House for many years and had a wide acquaintance with public men and the workings of legislative machinery. His advice was most helpful. I had already served with all the members of the Cabinet, which perhaps was one reason I found them so sympathetic.

Among its membership were men of great ability who have served their country with a capacity which I do not believe was ever exceeded by any former Cabinet officers.

A large amount was learned from George Harvey, Ambassador to England, concerning the European situation. He not only had a special aptitude for gathering and digesting information of that nature, but had been located at London for two years, where most of it centered.

I called in a great many people from all the different walks of life over the country. Among the first to come voluntarily were the veteran President and the Secretary of the American Federation of Labor, Mr. Gompers and Mr. Morrison. They brought a formal resolution expressive of personal regard for me and assurance of loyal support for the government.*

Farm organizations and business men, publishers, educators, and many others—all had to be consulted.

It has been my policy to seek information and advice wherever I could find it. I have never relied on any particular person to be my unofficial adviser. I have let the merits of each case and the soundness of all advice speak for themselves. My counselors have been those provided by the Constitution and the law.

Due largely to this careful preparation, my Message was well received. No other public utterance of mine had been given greater approbation.

Most of the praise was sincere. But there were some quarters in the opposing party where it was thought it would be good strategy to encourage my party to nominate me, thinking that it would be easy to accomplish my defeat. I do not know whether their judgment was wrong or whether they overdid the operation, so that when they stopped speaking in my praise they found they could not change the opinion of the people which they had helped to create.

I have seen a great many attempts at political strategy in my day and elaborate plans made to encompass the destruction of this or that public man. I cannot now think of any that did not react with overwhelming force upon the perpetrators, sometimes destroying them and sometimes giving their proposed victim an opportunity to demonstrate his courage, strength and

---

* The president of the American Federation of Labor (AFL) was Samuel Gompers, whom Governor Coolidge had faced down in the Boston police strike. The secretary was Frank Morrison. In the 1924 presidential election, the AFL endorsed the third-party candidate, Progressive Robert La Follette. Gompers died several weeks after that election, in which Coolidge won the presidency in his own right.

soundness, which increased his standing with the people and raised him to higher office.

There is only one form of political strategy in which I have any confidence, and that is to try to do the right thing and sometimes be able to succeed.

Many people at once began to speak about nominating me to lead my party in the next campaign. I did not take any position in relation to their efforts. Unless the nomination came to me in a natural way, rather than as the result of an artificial campaign, I did not feel it would be of any value.

The people ought to make their choice on a great question of that kind without the influence that could be exerted by a President in office.

After the favorable reception which was given to my Message, I stated at the Gridiron Dinner that I should be willing to be a candidate. The convention nominated me the next June by a vote which was practically unanimous.

With the exception of the occasion of my notification, I did not attend any partisan meetings or make any purely political speeches during the campaign. I spoke several times at the dedication of a monument, the observance of the anniversary of an historic event, at a meeting of some commercial body, or before some religious gathering. The campaign was magnificently managed by William M. Butler and as it progressed the final result became more and more apparent.

My own participation was delayed by the death of my son Calvin, which occurred on the seventh of July. He was a boy of much promise, proficient in his studies, with a scholarly mind, who had just turned sixteen.

He had a remarkable insight into things.

The day I became President he had just started to work in a tobacco field. When one of his fellow laborers said to him, "If my father was President I would not work in a tobacco field," Calvin replied, "If my father were your father, you would."*

After he was gone some one sent us a letter he had written about the same time to a young man who had congratulated him on being the first boy in the land. To this he had replied that he had done nothing, and so did not merit the title, which should go to "some boy who had distinguished himself through his own actions."

We do not know what might have happened to him under other circumstances, but if I had not been President he would not have raised a blister on his toe, which resulted in blood poisoning, playing lawn tennis in the South Grounds.

In his suffering he was asking me to make him well. I could not.

When he went the power and the glory of the Presidency went with him.†

The ways of Providence are often beyond our understanding. It seemed to me that the world had need of the work that it was probable he could do.

I do not know why such a price was exacted for occupying the White House.

Sustained by the great outpouring of sympathy from all over the nation, my wife and I bowed to the Supreme Will and

---

* When Coolidge assumed the presidency, the office was a besmirched institution, much ridiculed, especially as the details of the Teapot Dome scandal emerged. Coolidge took great pains to restore the reputation of the office, putting service before personal needs—including the needs of his family.

† Some historians have suggested that Coolidge gave up after his son's death, achieving little as president after the summer of 1924. The evidence, however, does not support such an assertion. Although President Coolidge deeply mourned Calvin Jr. and acknowledged the personal cost to him, in the final chapter of this autobiography, titled "Why I Did Not Choose to Run," Coolidge does not list Calvin Jr.'s death as one of the reasons he decided not to run again.

with such courage as we had went on in the discharge of our duties.

In less than two years my father followed him.

At his advanced age he had overtaxed his strength receiving the thousands of visitors who went to my old home at Plymouth. It was all a great satisfaction to him and he would not have had it otherwise.

When I was there and visitors were kept from the house for a short period, he would be really distressed in the thought that they could not see all they wished and he would go out where they were himself and mingle among them.

I knew for some weeks that he was passing his last days. I sent to bring him to Washington, but he clung to his old home.

It was a sore trial not to be able to be with him, but I had to leave him where he most wished to be. When his doctors advised me that he could survive only a short time I started to visit him, but he sank to rest while I was on my way.

For my personal contact with him during his last months I had to resort to the poor substitute of the telephone. When I reached home he was gone.

It costs a great deal to be President.

6

SOME OF THE DUTIES
OF THE PRESIDENT

A s I recall the mounting events of the years I spent in Washington, I appreciate how impossible it is to convey an adequate realization of the office of President. A few short paragraphs in the Constitution of the United States describe all his fundamental duties. Various laws passed over a period of nearly a century and a half have supplemented his authority. All of his actions can be analyzed. All of his goings and comings can be recited. The details of his daily life can be made known. The effect of his policies on his own country and on the world at large can be estimated. His methods of work, his associates, his place of abode, can all be described. But the relationship created by all these and more, which constitutes the magnitude of the office, does not yield to definition. Like the glory of a morning sunrise, it can only be experienced—it can not be told.

In the discharge of the duties of the office there is one rule of action more important than all others. It consists in never doing anything that some one else can do for you. Like many other good rules, it is proven by its exceptions. But it indicates a course that should be very strictly followed in order to prevent being so entirely devoted to trifling details that there will be little opportunity to give the necessary consideration to policies of larger importance.

Like some other rules, this one has an important corollary which must be carefully observed in order to secure success. It is not sufficient to entrust details to some one else. They must be entrusted to some one who is competent. The Presidency is primarily an executive office. It is placed at the apex of our system of government. It is a place of last resort to which all questions are brought that others have not been able to answer. The ideal way for it to function is to assign to the various positions men of sufficient ability so that they can solve all the problems that arise under their jurisdiction. If there is a troublesome situation in Nicaragua, a General McCoy can manage it. If we have differences with Mexico, a Morrow can compose them. If there is unrest in the Philippines, a Stimson can quiet them.* About a dozen able, courageous, reliable and experienced men in the House and the Senate can reduce the problem of legislation almost to a vanishing point.

While it is wise for the President to get all the competent advice possible, final judgments are necessarily his own. No one can share with him the responsibility for them. No one can

---

* Coolidge's references to individual negotiators here contrasts with his habitual emphasis, evident especially in his support of the Kellogg-Briand Pact, on solving international challenges through the avenues of international law. "General McCoy" is the U.S. Army's Frank R. McCoy, whom Coolidge appointed to supervise Nicaragua's 1928 presidential elections. "Morrow" is Ambassador Dwight Morrow, an eminent banker and Coolidge's old friend from Amherst College. "Stimson" is Henry L. Stimson, whom Coolidge named governor-general of the Philippines and who served in the cabinets of four presidents.

make his decisions for him. He stands at the center of things where no one else can stand. If others make mistakes, they can be relieved, and oftentimes a remedy can be provided. But he can not retire. His decisions are final and usually irreparable. This constitutes the appalling burden of his office. Not only the welfare of 120,000,000 of his countrymen, but oftentimes the peaceful relations of the world are entrusted to his keeping. At the turn of his hand the guns of an enormous fleet would go into action anywhere in the world, carrying the iron might of death and destruction. His appointment confers the power to administer justice, inflict criminal penalties, declare acts of state legislatures and of the Congress void, and sit in judgment over the very life of the nation. Practically all the civil and military authorities of the government, except the Congress and the courts, hold their office at his discretion. He appoints, and he can remove. The billions of dollars of government revenue are collected and expended under his direction. The Congress makes the laws, but it is the President who causes them to be executed. A power so vast in its implications has never been conferred upon any ruling sovereign.

Yet the President exercises his authority in accordance with the Constitution and the law. He is truly the agent of the people, performing such functions as they have entrusted to him. The Constitution specifically vests him with the executive power. Some Presidents have seemed to interpret that as an authorization to take any action which the Constitution, or perhaps the law, does not specifically prohibit. Others have considered that their powers extended only to such acts as were specifically authorized by the Constitution and the statutes. This has always seemed to me to be a hypothetical question, which it would be idle to attempt to determine in advance. It would appear to be the better practice to wait to decide each question on its merits as it arises. Jefferson is said to have entertained the opinion that there was no constitutional warrant for enlarging the territory of the United States, but when the actual facts confronted him he did not hesitate to negotiate the Louisiana Purchase. For all ordinary occasions the specific powers assigned to the President will be found sufficient to provide for the welfare of the country. That is all he needs.

All situations that arise are likely to be simplified, and many of them completely solved, by an application of the Constitution and the law. If what they require to be done, is done, there is no opportunity for criticism, and it would be seldom that anything better could be devised. A Commission once came to me with a proposal for adopting rules to regulate the conduct of its members. As they were evenly divided, each side wished me to decide against the other. They did this because, while it is always the nature of a Commissioner to claim that he is entirely independent of the President, he would usually welcome Presidential interference with any other Commissioner who does not agree with him. In this case it occurred to me that the Department of Justice should ascertain what the statute setting up this Commission required under the circumstances. A reference to the law disclosed that the Congress had specified the qualifications of the members of the Commission and that they could not by rule either enlarge or diminish the power of their individual members. So their problem was solved like many others by simply finding out what the law required.

Every day of the Presidential life is crowded with activities. When people not accustomed to Washington came to the office, or when I met them on some special occasion, they often remarked that it seemed to be my busy day, to which my stock reply came to be that all days were busy and there was little difference among them. It was my custom to be out of bed about six-thirty, except in the darkest mornings of winter. One of the doormen at the White House was an excellent barber, but I always preferred to shave myself with old-fashioned razors, which I knew how to keep in good condition. It was my intention to take a short walk before breakfast, which Mrs. Coolidge and I ate together in our rooms. For me there was fruit and about one-half cup of coffee, with a home-made cereal made from boiling together two parts of unground wheat with one part of rye. To this was added a roll and a strip of bacon, which went mostly to our dogs.

Soon after eight found me dictating in the White House library in preparation for some public utterance. This would go on for more than an hour, after which I began to receive callers at the office. Most of these came by appointment, but in addition to the average of six to eight who were listed there would be as many more from my Cabinet and the Congress, to whom I was always accessible. Each one came to me with a different problem requiring my decision, which was usually made at once. About twelve-fifteen those began to be brought in who were to be somewhat formally presented. At twelve-thirty the doors were opened, and a long line passed by who wished merely to shake hands with the President. On one occasion I shook hands with nineteen hundred in thirty-four minutes, which is probably my record. Instead of a burden, it was a pleasure and a relief to meet people in that way and listen to their greeting, which was often a benediction. It was at this same hour that the numerous groups assembled in the South Grounds, where I joined them for the photographs used for news purposes and permanent mementoes of their White House visit.

Lunch came at one o'clock, at which we usually had guests. It made an opportunity for giving our friends a little more attention than could be extended through a mere handshake.

About an hour was devoted to rest before returning to the office, where the afternoon was reserved for attention to the immense number of documents which pass over the desk of the President. These were all cleaned up each day. Before dinner another walk was in order, followed by exercises on some of the vibrating machines kept in my room. We gathered at the dinner table at seven o'clock and within three-quarters of an hour work would be resumed with my stenographer to continue until about ten o'clock.

The White House offices are under the direction of the Secretary to the President. They are the center of activities which are world-wide. Reports come in daily from heads of departments, from distant possessions, and from foreign diplomats and consular agents scattered all over the earth. A mass of correspondence, from the Congress, the officials of the states, and the general public, is constantly being received. All of this often reaches two thousand pieces in a day. Very much of it is sent at once to the Department to which it refers, from which an answer is sent direct to the writer. Other parts are sent to different members of the office staff; and some is laid before the President. While I signed many letters, I did not dictate many. After indicating the nature of the reply, it was usually put into form by some of the secretaries. A great many photographs were sent in to be inscribed, and a constant stream of autographs went to all who wrote for them.

At ten-thirty on Tuesdays and Fridays the Cabinet meetings were held. These were always very informal. Each member was asked if he had any problem he wished to lay before the President. When I first attended with President Harding at the beginning of a new administration these were rather numerous. Later, they decreased, as each member felt better able to solve his own problems. After entire freedom of discussion, but always without a vote of any kind, I was accustomed to announce what the decision should be. There never ought to be and never were marked differences of opinion in my Cabinet. As their duties were not to advise each other, but to advise the President, they could not disagree among themselves. I rarely failed to accept their recommendations. Sometimes they wished for larger appropriations than the state of the Treasury warranted, but they all cooperated most sincerely in the policy of economy and were content with such funds as I could assign to them.

The Secretary of State is the agency through which the President exercises his constitutional authority to deal with foreign relations. As this subject is a matter of constant interchange, he makes no annual report upon it. Other Cabinet officers make annual reports to the President on the whole conduct of their departments, which he transmits to the Congress. All the intercourse with foreign governments is carried on through the Secretary of State, and a national of a foreign country can not be received by the President unless the accredited diplomatic representative of his government has made an appointment for him through the State Department.

All foreign approaches to the President are through this Department. When an Ambassador or Minister is to present his credentials, the Undersecretary of State brings him to the White House and escorts him to the Green Room. After the President has taken his position standing in the Blue Room accompanied by his aides, the diplomat is then brought before him. He presents his letters with a short formal statement, to which the President responds in kind. When the mutual expressions of friendly interest and good will have been exchanged, the accompanying staff of the diplomat is brought in for presentation, after which he retires. Except when foreign officials are presented for an audience in this way, the etiquette of the White House requires that those who are present should remain until the President and the Mistress of the White House retire from the room.

A competent man is assigned from the State Department to have the management of the White House official social function. He has under him a considerable staff located in one of the basement rooms, known as the Social Bureau. They keep a careful list of all those who leave cards and of the officials who should be invited to receptions, which is constantly revised to meet changing conditions. While the President has supervision over all these functions, the most effective way to deal with them is to provide a capable Mistress of the White House. I have often been complimented on the choice which I made nearly twenty-five years ago. These functions were so much in the hands of Mrs. Coolidge that oftentimes I did not know what guests were to be present until I met them in the Blue Room just before going in to dinner.

These social functions are almost as much a part of the life of official Washington as a session of the Congress or a term of the Supreme Court. The season opens with the Cabinet dinner. Following this come the Diplomatic reception, the Diplomatic dinner, then the Judicial reception, the Supreme Court dinner, then the Congressional reception and the Speaker's dinner, with the last reception of the year tendered to the Army and Navy. About fifty guests assemble at the dinners, except that given to the diplomats, when the presence of the Ambassadors or Ministers, with their wives, of all countries represented in Washington brings the number up to about ninety. The Marine Band is in attendance on all these occasions. Following the dinners a short musical recital by famous artists is given in the East Room, to which many additional guests are invited.

A reception is a particularly colorful event. About thirty-five hundred invitations are issued. When the guests are assembled the President and his wife, preceded by his aides and followed by the Cabinet and his Secretary and their wives, go down the main staircase, pausing for a moment to receive the military salute of the band, and then pass to the Blue Room where the receptions are always held. When the foreign diplomats are present in their official dress, the scene is very brilliant. After all the presentations have been made, the President and his retinue return to the second floor. Immediately after this there is dancing in the East Room to furnish entertainment while the long line of cars comes up to take the guests home.

Whenever the prominent officials of foreign governments visit Washington, it is customary to receive them at a luncheon or dinner at the White House. When the Prince of Wales was here in 1924 we were in mourning, due to the loss of our son, so that he lunched with us informally without any other invited guests. When the Queen of Rumania came to Washington she was entertained at dinner. There have also been Princes of the reigning house of Japan and of Sweden, the Premier of France, the Governor General of Canada, the Presidents of the Irish Free State, of Cuba, and of Mexico, who have been received and entertained in some manner. Whenever an official gathering of foreigners, like the Panama Conference, convenes in Washington, the President and the Mistress of the White House tender them a reception and a dinner.

Besides these formal social gatherings, there were various afternoon teas and musicales, which I sometimes neglected, and usually one or two garden parties held in the South Grounds, one of which was for the disabled veterans who were patients in Washington hospitals. These parties were accompanied with band music and light refreshments, which always seemed to be appreciated by the veterans.

My personal social functions consisted of the White House

breakfasts, which were attended by fifteen to twenty-five members of the House and Senate and others, who gathered around my table at eight-thirty o'clock in the morning to partake of a meal which ended with wheat cakes and Vermont maple syrup. During the last session of the Congress I invited all the members of the Senate, all the chairmen and ranking Democratic members of the committees of the House, and finally had breakfast with the officers of both houses of the Congress. Although we did not undertake to discuss matters of public business at these breakfasts, they were productive of a spirit of good fellowship which was no doubt a helpful influence to the transaction of public business.

In addition to these White House events, the President and his wife go out to twelve official dinners. They begin with the Vice-President, go on among the ten members of the Cabinet, and close with the Speaker of the House. Aside from these, it is not customary for the President to accept the hospitality of any individuals. This is not from any desire on his part to be exclusive, but rather arises from an application of the principle of equality. The number of days in his term of office is limited. If he gave up all the time when he is not otherwise necessarily engaged, it is doubtful if he could find fifty evenings in a year when he could accept invitations. At once he would be confronted with the necessity of deciding which to accept and which to reject. If he served eight years, he could only touch the fringe of official Washington, even if he chose to disregard all the balance of the country. The only escape from an otherwise impossible situation is to observe the rule of refusing all social invitations.

The President stands at the head of all official and social rank in the nation. As he is Commander-in-Chief of the Army and Navy, all their officers are his subordinates. As he is the head of the government, he outranks all other public officials.

As the first citizen, he is placed at the top of the social scale. Wherever he goes, whenever he appears, he must be assigned the place of honor. It follows from this that he can not consistently attend a dinner or any other function given by some one else in honor of any other person. He can have ceremonies of his own at the White House, or outside, in which he recognizes the merit of others and bestows upon them appropriate honors. But his participation in any other occasion of such a nature is confined to sending an appropriate message.

It would make great confusion in all White House relations unless the rules of procedure were observed. If this were not done, the most ambitious and intruding would seize the place of honor, or it would be bestowed by favor. In both cases all official position would be ignored. In its working out, therefore, the adoption of rules which take no account of persons, but simply apply to places, is the only method which is in harmony with our spirit of equality. In its application it gives us more completely a government of laws and not of men.

As he is head of the government, charged with making appointments, and clothed with the executive power, the President has a certain responsibility for the conduct of all departments, commissions and independent bureaus. While I was willing to advise with any of these officers and give them any assistance in my power, I always felt they should make their own decisions and rarely volunteered any advice. Many applications are made requesting the President to seek to influence these bodies, and such applications were usually transmitted to them for their information without comment. Wherever they exercise judicial functions, I always felt that some impropriety might attach to any suggestions from me. The parties before them are entitled to a fair trial on the merits of their case and to have judgment rendered by those to whom both sides have presented their evidence.

If some one on the outside undertook to interfere, even if grave injustice was not done, the integrity of a commission which comes from a knowledge that it can be relied on to exercise its own independent judgment would be very much impaired.

I never hesitated to ask commissions to speed up their work and get their business done, but if they were not doing it correctly my remedy would be to supplant them with those who I thought would do better. At one time the Shipping Board adopted a resolution declaring their independence of the President and claiming they were responsible solely to the Congress. As I always considered they had a rather impossible task, I doubted whether any one could be very successful in its performance. If they wished to try to relieve me of its responsibility, I had no personal objection and would probably be saved from considerable criticism. But they found they could not carry on their work without the support of the President, so that some of them resigned and the remainder reestablished their contact with the White House, which was always open to them.

The practice which I followed in my relations with commissions and in the recognition of rank has been long established. President Jefferson seems to have entertained the opinion that even the Supreme Court should be influenced by his wishes and that failing in this a recalcitrant judge should be impeached by a complaisant Congress. This brought him into a sharp conflict with John Marshall, who resisted any encroachment upon the independence of the Court. In this controversy the position of Marshall has been vindicated. It is also said that at some of his official dinners President Jefferson left all his guests to the confusion of taking whatever seat they could find at his table. But this method did not survive the test of history. In spite of all his greatness, any one who had as many ideas as Jefferson was bound to find that some of them would not work. But this does not detract from the wisdom of his faith in the people and his constant insistence that they be left to manage their own affairs. His opposition to bureaucracy will bear careful analysis, and the country could stand a great deal more of its application. The trouble with us is that we talk about Jefferson but do not follow him. In his theory that the people should manage their government, and not be managed by it, he was everlastingly right.

Tradition and custom, it will be seen, are oftentimes determining factors in the Presidential office, as they are in all other walks of life. This is not because they are arbitrary or artificial, but because long experience has demonstrated that they are the best methods of dealing with human affairs. Things are done in a certain way after many repetitions show that way causes the least friction and is most likely to bring the desired result. While there are times when the people might enjoy the spectacular, in the end they will only be satisfied with accomplishments. The President gets the best advice he can find, uses the best judgment at his command, and leaves the event in the hands of Providence.

Everything that the President does potentially at least is of such great importance that he must be constantly on guard. This applies not only to himself, but to everybody about him. Not only in all his official actions, but in all his social intercourse, and even in his recreation and repose, he is constantly watched by a multitude of eyes to determine if there is anything unusual, extraordinary, or irregular, which can be set down in praise or in blame. Oftentimes trifling incidents, some insignificant action, an unfortunate phrase in an address, an injudicious letter, a lack of patience towards some one who presents an impossible proposition, too much attention to one person, or too little courtesy towards another, become magnified into the sensation of the hour. While such events finally sink into their proper place in history as too small for consideration, if they occur frequently they create an atmosphere of distraction that might seriously interfere with the conduct of public business which is really important.

It was my desire to maintain about the White House as far as possible an attitude of simplicity and not engage in anything that had an air of pretentious display. That was my conception of the great office. It carries sufficient power within itself, so that it does not require any of the outward trappings of pomp and splendor for the purpose of creating an impression. It has a dignity of its own which makes it self-sufficient. Of course, there should be proper formality, and personal relations should be conducted at all times with decorum and dignity, and in accordance with the best traditions of polite society. But there is no need of theatricals.

But, however much he may deplore it, the President ceases to be an ordinary citizen. In order to function at all he has to be surrounded with many safeguards. If these were removed for only a short time, he would be overwhelmed by the people who would surge in upon him. In traveling it would be agreeable to me to use the regular trains which are open to the public. I have done so once or twice. But I found it made great difficulty for the railroads. They reported that it was unsafe, because they could not take the necessary precautions. It therefore seemed best to run a second section, following a regular train, for the exclusive use of the President and his party. While the facilities of a private car have always been offered, I think they have only been used once, when one was needed for the better comfort of Mrs. Coolidge during her illness. Although I have not been given to much travel during my term of office, it has been sufficient, so that I am convinced the government should own a private car for the use of the President when he leaves Washington. The pressure on him is so great, the responsibilities are so heavy, that it is wise public policy in order to secure his best services to provide him with such ample facilities that he will be relieved as far as possible from all physical inconveniences.

It is not generally understood how much detail is involved in any journey of the President. One or two secret service men must go to the destination several days in advance. His line of travel and every street and location which he is to visit are carefully examined. The order of ceremonies has to be submitted for approval. Oftentimes the local police are inadequate, so that it is necessary to use some of the military or naval forces to assist them. Not only his aides and his personal physician, but also secret service men, some of his office force, and house servants, have to be in attendance. Quarters must also be provided for a large retinue of newspaper reporters and camera men who follow him upon all occasions. Every switch that he goes over is spiked down. Every freight train that he passes is stopped and every passenger train slowed down to ten miles per hour. While all of this proceeds smoothly, it requires careful attention to a great variety of details.

It has never been my practice to speak from rear platforms. The confusion is so great that few people could hear and it does not seem to me very dignified. When the President speaks it ought to be an event. The excuse for such appearances which formerly existed has been eliminated by the coming of the radio.* It is so often that the President is on the air that almost

---

* Coolidge was adept at exploiting new technologies, and radio was chief among them in the 1920s. He understood the importance of radio for reaching the American people directly and practiced the craft of communicating via that medium. Historian Jerry Wallace relates in his book *Calvin Coolidge: Our First Radio President* that Coolidge received training in "microphone manners" and that Coolidge's voice carried especially well over the airwaves. Over his five and a half years in office, Coolidge made more than forty radio addresses.

any one who wishes has ample opportunity to hear his voice. It has seemed more appropriate for Mrs. Coolidge and me to appear at the rear of the train where the people could see us. About the only time that I have spoken was at Bennington in September of 1928, where I expressed my affection and respect for the people of the state of Vermont, as I was passing through that town on my way back to Washington. I found that the love I had for the hills where I was born touched a responsive chord in the heart of the whole nation.

One of the most appalling trials which confront a President is the perpetual clamor for public utterances. Invitations are constant and pressing. They come by wire, by mail, and by delegations. No event of importance is celebrated anywhere in the United States without inviting him to come to deliver an oration. When others are enjoying a holiday, he is expected to make a public appearance in order to entertain and instruct by a formal address. There are a few public statements that he does not deliver in person, like proclamations, and messages, which go to the Congress, either reporting his views on the state of the Union in his Annual Message or giving his reasons for rejecting legislation in a veto. These productions vary in length. My Annual Message would be about twelve thousand words. My speeches would average a little over three thousand words. In the course of a year the entire number reaches about twenty, which probably represents an output of at least seventy-five thousand words.

This kind of work is very exacting. It requires the most laborious and extended research and study, and the most careful and painstaking thought. Each word has to be weighed in the realization that it is a Presidential utterance which will be dissected at home and abroad to discover its outward meaning and any possible hidden implications. Before it is finished it is thoroughly examined by one or two of my staff, and oftentimes by a member of the Cabinet. It is not difficult for me to deliver an address. The difficulty lies in its preparation. This is an important part of the work of a President which he can not escape. It is inherent in the office.*

A great many presents come to the White House, which are all cherished, not so much for their intrinsic value as because they are tokens of esteem and affection. Almost everything that can be eaten comes. We always know what to do with that. But some of the pets that are offered us are more of a problem. I have a beautiful black-haired bear that was brought all the way from Mexico in a truck, and a pair of live lion cubs now grown up, and a small species of hippopotamus which came from South Africa. These and other animals and birds have been placed in the zoological quarters in Rock Creek Park. We always had more dogs than we could take care of. My favorites were the white collies, which became so much associated with me that they are enshrined in my bookplate, where they will live as long as our country endures. One of them, Prudence Prim, was especially attached to Mrs. Coolidge. We lost her in the Black Hills. She lies out there in the shadow of Bear Butte where the Indians told me the Great Spirit came to commune with his children.† One was my companion, Rob Roy. He was a stately gentleman of great courage and fidelity. He loved to bark

---

* Coolidge was, in fact, the last president to write most of his own speeches. The text of several of his important addresses can be found in the appendix of this book. Many other Coolidge speeches can be found on the website of the Calvin Coolidge Presidential Foundation, coolidgefoundation.org.

† The Coolidges made the Black Hills of South Dakota the site of the 1927 Summer White House. During their stay, Coolidge was honored by the Sioux tribe with the honorary title "Chief Leading Eagle." Earlier, in 1924, Coolidge had signed the Indian Citizenship Act, making every Native American a citizen of the United States.

from the second-story windows and around the South Grounds. Nights he remained in my room and afternoons went with me to the office. His especial delight was to ride with me in the boats when I went fishing. So although I know he would bark for joy as the grim boatman ferried him across the dark waters of the Styx, yet his going left me lonely on the hither shore.

As I left office I realized that the more I had seen of the workings of the Federal government the more respect I came to have for it. It is carried on by hundreds of thousands of people. Some prove incompetent. A very few are tempted to become disloyal to their trust. But the great rank and file of them are of good ability, conscientious, and faithful public servants. While some are paid more than they would earn in private life, there are great throngs who are serving at a distinct personal sacrifice. Among the higher officials this is almost always true. The service they perform entitles them to approbation and honor.

The Congress has sometimes been a sore trial to Presidents. I did not find it so in my case. Among them were men of wonderful ability and veteran experience. I think they made their decisions with an honest purpose to serve their country. The membership of the Senate changed very much by reason of those who sacrificed themselves for public duty. Of all public officials with whom I have ever been acquainted, the work of a Senator of the United States is by far the most laborious. About twenty of them died during the eight years I was in Washington.

Sometimes it would seem for a day that either the House or the Senate had taken some unwise action, but if it was not corrected on the floor where it occurred it was usually remedied in the other chamber. I always found the members of both parties willing to confer with me and disposed to treat my recommendations fairly. Most of the differences could be adjusted by personal discussion. Sometimes I made an appeal direct to the country by stating my position at the newspaper conferences. I adopted that course in relation to the Mississippi Flood Control Bill. As it passed the Senate it appeared to be much too extravagant in its rule of damages and its proposed remedy. The press began a vigorous discussion of the subject, which caused the House greatly to modify the bill, and in conference a measure that was entirely fair and moderate was adopted. On other occasions I appealed to the country more privately, enlisting the influence of labor and trade organizations upon the Congress in behalf of some measures in which I was interested. That was done in the case of the tax bill of 1928. As it passed the House, the reductions were so large that the revenue necessary to meet the public expenses would not have been furnished. By quietly making this known to the Senate, and enlisting support for that position among their constituents, it was possible to secure such modification of the measure that it could be adopted without greatly endangering the revenue.

But a President cannot, with success, constantly appeal to the country. After a time he will get no response. The people have their own affairs to look after and can not give much attention to what the Congress is doing. If he takes a position, and stands by it, ultimately it will be adopted. Most of the policies set out in my first Annual Message have become law, but it took several years to get action on some of them.

One of the most perplexing and at the same time most important functions of the President is the making of appointments. In some few cases he acts alone, but usually they are made with the advice and consent of the Senate. It is the practice to consult Senators of his own party before making an appointment from their state. In choosing persons for service over the whole or any considerable portion of a single state, it is customary to rely almost entirely on the party Senators from that state for recommendations. It is not possible to find men who are perfect. Selection always has to be limited to human beings, whatever choice is made. It is therefore always possible to point out defects. The supposition that no one should be appointed who has had experience in the field which he is to supervise is extremely detrimental to the public service. An Interstate Commerce Commissioner is much better qualified, if he knows something about transportation. A Federal Trade Commissioner can render much better service if he has had a legal practice which extended into large business transactions. The assertion of those who contend that persons accepting a government appointment would betray their trust in favor of former associates can be understood only on the supposition that those who make it feel that their own tenure of public office is for the purpose of benefiting themselves and their friends.

Every one knows that where the treasure is, there will the heart be also. When a man has invested his personal interest and reputation in the conduct of a public office, if he goes wrong it will not be because of former relations, but because he is a bad man. The same interests that reached him would reach any bad man, irrespective of former life history. What we need in appointive positions is men of knowledge and experience who have sufficient character to resist temptations. If that standard is maintained, we need not be concerned about their former activities. If it is not maintained, all the restrictions on their past employment that can be conceived will be of no avail.

The more experience I have had in making appointments, the more I am convinced that attempts to put limitations on the appointing power are a mistake. It should be possible to choose a well qualified person wherever he can be found. When restrictions are placed on residence, occupation, or profession, it almost always happens that some one is found who is universally admitted to be the best qualified, but who is eliminated by the artificial specifications. So long as the Senate has the power to reject nominations, there is little danger that a President would abuse his authority if he were given the largest possible freedom in his choices. The public service would be improved if all vacancies were filled by simply appointing the best ability and character that can be found. That is what is done in private business. The adoption of any other course handicaps the government in all its operations.

In determining upon all his actions, however, the President has to remember that he is dealing with two different minds. One is the mind of the country, largely intent upon its own personal affairs, and, while not greatly interested in the government, yet desirous of seeing it conducted in an orderly and dignified manner for the advancement of the public welfare. Those who compose this mind wish to have the country prosperous and are opposed to unjust taxation and public extravagance. At the same time they have a patriotic pride which moves them with so great a desire to see things well done that they are willing to pay for it. They gladly contribute their money to place the United States in the lead. In general, they represent the public opinion of the land.

But they are unorganized, formless, and inarticulate. Against a compact and well drilled minority they do not appear to be very effective. They are nevertheless the great power in our government. I have constantly appealed to them and have seldom failed in enlisting their support. They are the court of last resort and their decisions are final.

They are, however, the indirect rather than the direct power. The immediate authority with which the President has to deal is vested in the political mind. In order to get things done he has to work through that agency. Some of our Presidents have appeared to lack comprehension of the political mind. Although I have been associated with it for many years, I always found difficulty in understanding it. It is a strange mixture of vanity and timidity, of an obsequious attitude at one time and a delusion of grandeur at another time, of the most selfish preferment combined with the most sacrificing patriotism. The political mind is the product of men in public life who have been twice spoiled. They have been spoiled with praise and they have been spoiled with abuse. With them nothing is natural, everything is artificial. A few rare souls escape these influences and maintain a vision and a judgment that are unimpaired. They are a great comfort to every President and a great service to their country. But they are not sufficient in number so that the public business can be transacted like a private business.

It is because in their hours of timidity the Congress becomes subservient to the importunities of organized minorities that the President comes more and more to stand as the champion of the rights of the whole country. Organizing such minorities has come to be a well-recognized industry at Washington. They are oftentimes led by persons of great ability, who display much skill in bringing their influences to bear on the Congress. They have ways of securing newspaper publicity, deluging Senators and Representatives with petitions and overwhelming them with imprecations that are oftentimes decisive in securing the passage of bills. While much of this legislation is not entirely bad, almost all of it is excessively expensive. If it were not for the rules of the House and the veto power of the President, within two years these activities would double the cost of the government.

Under our system the President is not only the head of the government, but is also the head of his party. The last twenty years have witnessed a decline in party spirit and a distinct weakening in party loyalty. While an independent attitude on the part of the citizen is not without a certain public advantage, yet it is necessary under our form of government to have political parties. Unless some one is a partisan, no one can be an independent. The Congress is organized entirely in accordance with party policy. The parties appeal to the voters in behalf of their platforms. The people make their choice on those issues. Unless those who are elected on the same party platform associate themselves together to carry out its provisions, the election becomes a mockery. The independent voter who has joined with others in placing a party nominee in office finds his efforts were all in vain, if the person he helps elect refuses or neglects to keep the platform pledges of his party.

Many occasions arise in the Congress when party lines are very properly disregarded, but if there is to be a reasonable government proceeding in accordance with the express mandate of the people, and not merely at the whim of those who happen to be victorious at the polls, on all the larger and important issues there must be party solidarity. It is the business of the President as party leader to do the best he can to see that the declared party platform purposes are translated into legislative and administrative action. Oftentimes I secured support from those without my party and had opposition from those within my party, in attempting to keep my platform pledges.

Such a condition is entirely anomalous. It leaves the President as the sole repository of party responsibility. But it is one of the reasons that the Presidential office has grown in popular estimation and favor, while the Congress has declined. The country feels that the President is willing to assume responsibility, while his party in the Congress is not. I have never felt it was my duty to attempt to coerce Senators or Representatives, or to take reprisals. The people sent them to Washington. I felt I had discharged my duty when I had done the best I could with them. In this way I avoided almost entirely a personal opposition, which I think was of more value to the country than to attempt to prevail through arousing personal fear.

Under our system it ought to be remembered that the power to initiate policies has to be centralized somewhere. Unless the party leaders exercising it can depend on loyalty and organization support, the party in which it is reposed will become entirely ineffective. A party which is ineffective will soon be discarded. If a party is to endure as a serviceable instrument of government for the country, it must possess and display a healthy spirit of party loyalty. Such a manifestation in the Congress would do more than anything else to rehabilitate it in the esteem and confidence of the country.

It is natural for man to seek power. It was because of this trait of human nature that the founders of our institutions provided a system of checks and balances. They placed all their public officers under constitutional limitations. They had little fear of the courts and were inclined to regard legislative bodies as the natural champions of their liberties. They were very apprehensive that the executive might seek to exercise arbitrary powers. Under our Constitution such fears seldom have been well founded. The President has tended to become the champion of the people because he is held solely responsible for his acts, while in the Congress where responsibility is divided it has developed that there is much greater danger of arbitrary action.

It has therefore become increasingly imperative that the President should resist any encroachment upon his constitutional powers. One of the most important of these is the power of appointment. The Constitution provides that he shall nominate, and by and with the advice and consent of the Senate appoint. A constant pressure is exerted by the Senators to make their own nominations and the Congress is constantly proposing laws which undertake to deprive the President of the appointive power. Different departments and bureaus are frequently supporting measures that would make them self-perpetuating bodies to which no appointments could be made that they did not originate. While I have always sought cooperation and advice, I have likewise resisted these efforts, sometimes by refusing to adopt recommendations and sometimes by the exercise of the veto power. One of the farm relief bills, and later a public health measure, had these clearly unconstitutional limitations on the power of appointment. In the defense of the rights and liberties of the people it is necessary for the President to resist all encroachments upon his lawful authority.

All of these trials and encouragements come to each President. It is impossible to explain them. Even after passing through the Presidential office, it still remains a great mystery. Why one person is selected for it and many others are rejected can not be told. Why people respond as they do to its influence seems to be beyond inquiry. Any man who has been placed in the White House can not feel that it is the result of his own exertions or his own merit. Some power outside and beyond him becomes manifest through him. As he contemplates the workings of his office, he comes to realize with an increasing sense of humility that he is but an instrument in the hands of God.

7

WHY I DID NOT CHOOSE TO RUN

erhaps I have already indicated some of the reasons why
I did not desire to be a candidate to succeed myself.
The Presidential office takes a heavy toll of those
who occupy it and those who are dear to them. While we should
not refuse to spend and be spent in the service of our country,
it is hazardous to attempt what we feel is beyond our strength
to accomplish.

I had never wished to run in 1928 and had determined to
make a public announcement at a sufficiently early date so that
the party would have ample time to choose some one else. An
appropriate occasion for that announcement seemed to be the
fourth anniversary of my taking office. The reasons I can give
may not appear very convincing, but I am confident my decision
was correct.

My personal and official relations have all been peculiarly
pleasant. The Congress has not always done all that I wished,
but it has done very little that I did not approve. So far as I can

judge, I have been especially fortunate in having the approbation of the country.

But irrespective of the third-term policy, the Presidential office is of such a nature that it is difficult to conceive how one man can successfully serve the country for a term of more than eight years.

While I am in favor of continuing the long-established custom of the country in relation to a third term for a President, yet I do not think that the practice applies to one who has succeeded to part of a term as Vice-President. Others might argue that it does, but I doubt if the country would so consider it.*

Although my own health has been practically perfect, yet the duties are very great and ten years would be a very heavy strain. It would be especially long for the Mistress of the White House. Mrs. Coolidge has been in more than usual good health, but I doubt if she could have stayed there for ten years without some danger of impairment of her strength.

A President should not only not be selfish, but he ought to avoid the appearance of selfishness. The people would not have confidence in a man that appeared to be grasping for office.

It is difficult for men in high office to avoid the malady of self-delusion. They are always surrounded by worshipers. They are constantly, and for the most part sincerely, assured of their greatness.

They live in an artificial atmosphere of adulation and exaltation which sooner or later impairs their judgment. They are in grave danger of becoming careless and arrogant.

The chances of having wise and faithful public service are

---

* In 1951, ratification of the Twenty-Second Amendment would enshrine the two-term limit on presidents. Coolidge's assessment turned out to be correct: according to this constitutional amendment, a vice president who serves less than two years of the former president's term is eligible to be elected to two terms in his or her own right.

increased by a change in the Presidential office after a moderate length of time.

It is necessary for the head of the nation to differ with many people who are honest in their opinions. As his term progresses, the number who are disappointed accumulates. Finally, there is so large a body who have lost confidence in him that he meets a rising opposition which makes his efforts less effective.

In the higher ranges of public service men appear to come forward to perform a certain duty. When it is performed their work is done. They usually find it impossible to readjust themselves in the thought of the people so as to pass on successfully to the solution of new public problems.

An examination of the records of those Presidents who have served eight years will disclose that in almost every instance the latter part of their term has shown very little in the way of constructive accomplishment. They have often been clouded with grave disappointments.

While I had a desire to be relieved of the pretensions and delusions of public life, it was not because of any attraction of pleasure or idleness.

We draw our Presidents from the people. It is a wholesome thing for them to return to the people. I came from them. I wish to be one of them again.

Although all our Presidents have had back of them a good heritage of blood, very few have been born to the purple. Fortunately, they are not supported at public expense after leaving office, so they are not expected to set an example encouraging to a leisure class.*

---

* Congress would change this arrangement in 1958 by passing the Former Presidents Act. By law, former presidents now receive lifetime pensions, Secret Service protection, staff and office expenses, and health insurance.

They have only the same title to nobility that belongs to all our citizens, which is the one based on achievement and character, so they need not assume superiority. It is becoming for them to engage in some dignified employment where they can be of service as others are.

Our country does not believe in idleness. It honors hard work. I wanted to serve the country again as a private citizen.

In making my public statement I was careful in the use of words. There were some who reported that they were mystified as to my meaning when I said, "I do not choose to run."*

Although I did not know it at the time, months later I found that Washington said practically the same thing. Certainly he said no more in his Farewell Address, where he announced that "choice and prudence" invited him to retire.

There were others who constantly demanded that I should state that if nominated I would refuse to accept. Such a statement would not be in accordance with my conception of the requirements of the Presidential office. I never stated or formulated in my own mind what I should do under such circumstances, but I was determined not to have that contingency arise.

I therefore sent the Secretary to the President, Everett Sanders, a man of great ability and discretion, to Kansas City with instructions to notify several of the leaders of state delegations not to vote for me. Had I not done so, I am told, I should have been nominated.

---

* Some observers wondered whether Coolidge's wording left matters intentionally ambiguous. Was he suggesting he would accede to a "draft Coolidge" movement? But Coolidge's wording reflected not indecision but rather the independence the Vermonter cherished. "I do not choose" emphasized Coolidge's authority to make the decision on his own. Edmund Starling, the Secret Service agent who spent countless hours with Coolidge, reflected, "Nothing is more sacred to a New England Yankee than this privilege as an individual to make up his own mind."

The report that he had talked with me on the telephone after his arrival, and I had told him I would not accept if nominated, was pure fabrication. I had no communication with him of any kind after he left Washington and did not give him any such instruction or message at any time.

I thought if I could prevent being nominated, which I was able to do, it would never be necessary for me to decide the other question. But in order to be perfectly free, I sent this notice, so that if I declined no one could say I had misled him into supposing that I was willing to receive his vote.

I felt sure that the party and the country were in so strong a position that they could easily nominate and elect some other candidate. The events have confirmed my judgment.

In the primary campaign I was careful to make it known that I was not presenting any candidate. The friends of several of them no doubt represented that their candidate was satisfactory to me, which was true as far as it went.

I can conceive a situation in which a President might be warranted in exercising the influence of his office in selecting his successor. That condition did not exist in the last primary. The party had plenty of material, which was available, and the candidate really should be the choice of the people themselves. This is especially so now that so many of the states have laws for the direct expression of the choice of the voters.

A President in office can do very much about the nomination of his successor, because of his influence with the convention, but the feeling that he had forced a choice would place the nominee under a heavy handicap.

When the convention assembles it is almost certain that it will look about to see what candidate has made the largest popular showing, and unless some peculiar disqualification develops it will nominate him.

That was what happened in the last convention, although no one had a majority when the convention assembled.

A strong group of the party in and outside of the Senate made the mistake of undertaking to oppose Mr. Hoover with a large number of local candidates, which finally resulted in their not developing enough strength for any particular candidate to make a showing sufficient to impress the convention.

Although I did not intimate in any way that I would not accept the nomination, when I sent word to the heads of certain unpledged state delegations not to vote for me, they very naturally turned to Mr. Hoover, which brought about his nomination on the first ballot.*

The Presidential office differs from everything else. Much of it cannot be described, it can only be felt. After I had considered the reasons for my being a candidate on the one side and on the other, I could not say that any of them moved me with compelling force.

My election seemed assured. Nevertheless, I felt it was not best for the country that I should succeed myself. A new impulse is more likely to be beneficial.

It was therefore my privilege, after seeing my administration so strongly indorsed by the country, to retire voluntarily from the greatest experience that can come to mortal man. In that way, I believed I could best serve the people who have honored me and the country which I love.

---

* Coolidge had a somewhat complicated relationship with the eventual Republican nominee—his secretary of commerce, Herbert Hoover. Coolidge respected Hoover's work habits but referred derisively to his commerce secretary as "Wonder Boy" for Hoover's faith in government action. Although Hoover campaigned in 1928 by promising a "continuation of Coolidge policies," Coolidge understood that Hoover's activism would set him on a different path.

THE END

BY THE HONORABLE JAMES H. DOUGLAS

C all me biased, but, as a rule, I prefer a governor to serve as president.

Both are executive roles, and, although nothing is perfectly comparable, serving as governor is the nearest form of public-sector experience to being president. Governors and presidents lead large, complex organizations. They constitute one of three coordinate and equal branches of government. They're charged with formulating policy, planning for the future, and carrying out laws enacted by legislators.

Governors and presidents are symbolic leaders, offering cheers at times of triumph and serving as consolers-in-chief when tragedy strikes. These executives are heads of state as well as of government. They must make the trains run on time, but they are also the public faces of the jurisdictions they serve.

The American people recognized these qualities in Calvin Coolidge when they elected him vice president. Coolidge came to national attention through his steady hand in addressing the Boston police strike the previous year. He calmly reviewed the applicable laws; consulted experienced officials, past and present; and followed a course that ended the crisis. Importantly, he acted in accord with the dictates of his conscience.

The strike is often cited as an example of successful executive leadership and the power of determination. Coolidge relates details of the episode in this autobiography—including a part of the story that is not widely known. Employees of the electric plant, supplying all the power to the city of Boston, threatened to join the police officers in walking off the job. Just as Governor Coolidge had ordered other law-enforcement agencies and the State Guard to provide support during the police strike, he had a backup plan for a second walkout, too: naval electricians standing by on a vessel just offshore.

Perhaps that's among the qualities most essential for an executive: planning ahead, anticipating what crises may arise, contemplating worst-case scenarios, and marshaling the resources required to confront them. I spent many hours in tabletop exercises, reviewing the preparedness of our emergency management team and ensuring that my cabinet appointees were ready for whatever may come. Preparation, emergency drills, and formulating plans for any contingency can make all the difference.

This new edition of Calvin Coolidge's autobiography emerges as the world endures a pandemic that has taken thousands of lives and adversely affected many more. The only certainty over time seems to be that some disaster will strike: it may be natural or unnatural, but the nation, state, or city that has prepared will be better for it.

That's part of the job description of a governor. I'd rather have someone who has managed a crisis, or at least prepared for one, leading our country.

James H. Douglas served as governor of Vermont from 2003 to 2011.

BY JENNIFER COOLIDGE HARVILLE

"For almost a quarter of a century she has borne with my infirmities, and I have rejoiced in her graces."

It was in this poetic fashion that, in the pages of this autobiography, President Calvin Coolidge described his wife. First Lady Grace Coolidge, my great-grandmother, indeed was a clever and extraordinary woman. Grace's service to her family and country earned the esteem of her contemporaries and contributed in important ways to the many achievements President Coolidge secured for the American people.

Grace Anna Goodhue was born January 3, 1879, in Burlington, Vermont, to Andrew and Lemira Goodhue. A graduate of the University of Vermont, Grace was the first first lady to complete college. Grace then moved to Northampton, Massachusetts, to study instruction of the deaf at the Clarke School. Later she had the honor of entertaining Helen Keller at the White House. She dedicated her entire life to working with the deaf community.

Grace met my great-grandfather Calvin in Northampton. After a brief courtship, they married on October 4, 1905, at the home of Grace's parents in Burlington. The pair set up house in half of a modest two-family duplex on Northampton's Massasoit Street. They lived in this house during Calvin's political years in Massachusetts. My great-grandparents had a strong and loving bond. About their marriage, Calvin wrote "the plain facts" were that he and Grace "thought we were made for each other."

Calvin and Grace welcomed their first son, John Coolidge—my grandfather—in September 1906. Their second son, Calvin Coolidge Jr., arrived in April 1908. By this time the elder Calvin was a lawmaker serving in the Massachusetts House of Representatives. Grace took primary responsibility for raising the two boys. Her devotion to the family allowed Calvin to pursue his career in law and politics, which eventually led to the White House. Grace lived the American suffrage movement: She voted in the first national election where women enjoyed the franchise. It must have been a special thrill to see her husband's name on that 1920 ballot as candidate for vice president.

When the Coolidges arrived at the White House, Grace expected the furnishings to reflect its previous residents, and it saddened her to find so little original furniture. At Grace's request, Congress passed a joint resolution to authorize people to donate historical gifts to recognize the President's House as a functioning museum. The White House Green Room was refurbished under this plan.

My great-grandmother inspired faith in the Coolidge family. Grace led the family's attendance at the Edwards Church in Northampton and oversaw her sons' religious education. Her beautiful singing voice helped strengthen the congregation at every church the family attended. Even in the most difficult times, Grace maintained her composure, relying on her faith. After the sudden death of Calvin Jr., Grace donned white for the mourning period and encouraged her family to carry on.

Primary among Grace's duties was serving as hostess in chief. She expressed pleasure at serving in this role: "In no sense does it overwhelm me," she wrote to her Pi Beta Phi sorority sisters. "Rather does it inspire me to increase my energy and I am so filled with the desire to measure up to this God-given task that I can almost feel strength poured into me." The extrovert Grace entertained with ease—a skill especially valuable as a foil to her husband's quiet demeanor. Grace loved music and joyfully hosted the White House musicales, at which the famous composer and pianist Sergei Rachmaninoff performed on three separate occasions. Grace supported the Red Cross by regularly visiting Walter Reed Hospital and hosting World War I disabled veterans at the White House. Her advocacy continued after her tenure as first lady. During World War II, she assisted in the production of surgical dressing for the Red Cross, supervised civilian defense efforts, and lent a hand in organizing gift drives to soldiers serving far from home.

As first lady, Grace was always accessible. She famously enjoyed brisk morning walks around Washington. She was an icon of fashion, but also down to earth. She had a passion for America's favorite pastime, earning her the nickname "The First Lady of Baseball." Grace also loved animals, keeping many pets, including dogs, cats, and birds, while at 1600 Pennsylvania Avenue. A raccoon, Rebecca, sent one year to be part of the Coolidges' Thanksgiving meal, was instead adopted as a family pet. She enjoyed hosting the annual lighting of the White House Christmas Tree and had fun showing Rebecca the Raccoon to the children at the annual Easter Egg Roll. In Grace, the American people saw a first lady, and indeed a first family, to whom they could relate.

The first lady outlived the president by nearly a quarter century. Grace spent her golden years in Northampton, traveling some, including a trip to Europe in 1936, but mostly dedicating herself to her community and family. She served as president of the board of the Clarke School for nearly twenty years. She especially enjoyed spending time with her son John and his wife, Florence, and her granddaughters, Cynthia and Lydia (my mother), whom she lovingly referred to as her "Precious Four."

Grace died peacefully in her sleep on July 8, 1957. Eulogizing the former first lady, the *New York Times* described Grace as "warm, outgoing, understanding," and wrote that Calvin "could not have picked a bride who would more successfully fill the role of First Lady." She rests next to generations of our family in the town cemetery of Plymouth Notch, Vermont.

Jennifer Coolidge Harville is the great-granddaughter of President Calvin Coolidge and First Lady Grace Coolidge.

BY CHRISTOPHER COOLIDGE JETER

M y grandfather John Coolidge was the surviving son of President Calvin Coolidge. Grandfather had a great command of the English language. He always seemed to have the right words at the right moments. I imagine that trait was due in part to his father, my great-grandfather Calvin Coolidge, who was also skilled in communication despite his reputation for brevity.

Another trait that these two men had in common was keeping a low profile. Neither one sought the spotlight or desired any special attention. I recall a time when I was assisting my grandfather tidying up around the family grave site in Plymouth. A visitor stopped by and, assuming we were cemetery caretakers, commented that it must be quite an honor for us to care for a presidential grave site. We agreed it was and just kept on working.

In my opinion, Calvin Coolidge's character was one of his strongest qualities. Some of his character and values were shaped by his parents and grandparents in his childhood. Some formed later in life during his years of public service. There are many notable parts of this autobiography, and it is difficult to point out just a few, but here are several passages that convey President Coolidge's character.

His memories as a young boy of his father:

> *The lines he laid out were true and straight, and the curves regular. The work he did endured. If there was any physical requirement of country life which he could not perform, I do not know what it was. From watching him and assisting him, I gained an intimate knowledge of all this kind of work.*

His thoughts on his reaction to the Boston police strike:

> *The right thing to do never requires any subterfuges, it is always simple and direct.*

Reflecting on the presidency:

> *It is a great advantage to a President, and a major source of safety to the country, for him to know that he is not a great man. When a man begins to feel that he is the only one who can lead in this republic, he is guilty of treason to the spirit of our institutions.*

His decision not to run again for president in 1928:

> *We draw our Presidents from the people. It is a wholesome thing for them to return to the people. I came from them. I wish to be one of them again.*

Strong character is still much needed today. Although Calvin Coolidge in his final years commented that he no longer fit with the times, it would be good to have a few Calvins around today. I am proud to be part of the family and help carry on some of the traditions, including maintaining land that has been in my family for eight generations.

I hope you have enjoyed reading this autobiography and getting a sense of who Calvin Coolidge was, directly from the man himself. If you ever find yourself in Vermont, please take the opportunity to tour the historic site in Plymouth Notch.

Christopher Coolidge Jeter is the great-grandson of President Calvin Coolidge and First Lady Grace Coolidge.

APPENDIX

SELECT SPEECHES OF CALVIN COOLIDGE

Calvin Coolidge devoted much time to his speeches and only rarely allowed others to write them. Coolidge once complimented the portraitist Ercole Cartotto for the collection of paintings Cartotto would leave behind. To show Cartotto he understood, Coolidge waved an arm toward a bookshelf that held volumes of his own speeches. "These are my paintings," the president said.

Like his autobiography, Coolidge's speeches reveal his talents as a writer and thinker. Here you will find several important addresses Coolidge gave. You can read hundreds of others on the website of the Calvin Coolidge Presidential Foundation, at coolidgefoundation.org.
—Amity Shlaes and Matthew Denhart

HAVE FAITH IN MASSACHUSETTS
JANUARY 7, 1914

This speech, which Coolidge delivered on becoming president of the Massachusetts senate, marked a turning point for the politician from

*western Massachusetts. The address was well received ("The effect
was beyond my expectation," Coolidge writes in this autobiography)
and established Coolidge as an important figure statewide. Later it
helped make him a national figure: in 1919, "Have Faith in Massachusetts" became the title piece in a widely distributed collection of
Coolidge speeches.*

*Here Coolidge offers insight into his political and social philoso-
phy, including his views on federalism, representative democracy, the
limitations of government, and the spiritual foundations of liberty.*

Honorable Senators:

I thank you, with gratitude for the high honor given, with
appreciation for the solemn obligations assumed, I thank you.

The commonwealth is one. We are all members of one
body. The welfare of the weakest and the welfare of the most
powerful are inseparably bound together. Industry cannot flourish if labor languish. Transportation cannot prosper if manufac-
tures decline. The general welfare cannot be provided for in
any one act, but it is well to remember that the benefit of one
is the benefit of all, and the neglect of one is the neglect of
all. The suspension of one man's dividends is the suspension of
another man's pay envelope.

Men do not make laws. They do but discover them. Laws
must be justified by something more than the will of the majority. They must rest on the eternal foundation of righteousness.
That state is most fortunate in its form of government which
has the aptest instruments for the discovery of laws. The lat-
est, most modern, and nearest perfect system that statesmanship
has devised is representative government. Its weakness is the
weakness of us imperfect human beings who administer it. Its
strength is that even such administration secures to the people
more blessings than any other system ever produced.

No nation has discarded it and retained liberty. Representative government must be preserved. Courts are established, not to determine the popularity of a cause, but to adjudicate and enforce rights. No litigant should be required to submit his case to the hazard and expense of a political campaign. No judge should be required to seek or receive political rewards. The courts of Massachusetts are known and honored wherever men love justice. Let their glory suffer no diminution at our hands. The electorate and judiciary cannot combine. A hearing means a hearing. When the trial of causes goes outside the court room, Anglo Saxon constitutional government ends. The people cannot look to legislation generally for success. Industry, thrift, character are not conferred by act or resolve.

Government cannot relieve from toil. It can provide no substitute for the rewards of service. It can, of course, care for the defective and recognize distinguished merit. The normal must care for themselves. Self-government means self-support. Man is born into the universe with a personality that is his own. He has a right that is founded upon the constitution of the universe to have property that is his own. Ultimately, property rights and personal rights are the same thing. The one cannot be preserved if the other be violated. Each man is entitled to his rights and the rewards of his service be they never so large or never so small.

History reveals no civilized people among whom there were not a highly educated class and large aggregations of wealth, represented usually by the clergy and the nobility. Inspiration has always come from above. Diffusion of learning has come down from the university to the common school; the kindergarten is last. No one would now expect to aid the common school by abolishing higher education. It may be that the diffusion of wealth works in an analogous way. As the little red schoolhouse is builded in the college, it may be that the fostering and protection of large aggregations of wealth are the only foundation on which to build the prosperity of the whole people. Large profits mean large payrolls. But profits must be the result of service performed. In no land are there so many and such large aggregations of wealth as here; in no land do they perform larger service; in no land will the work of a day bring so large a reward in material and spiritual welfare.

Have faith in Massachusetts. In some unimportant detail some other States may surpass her, but in the general results, there is no place on earth where the people secure, in a larger measure, the blessings of organized government, and nowhere can those functions more properly be termed self-government. Do the day's work. If it be to protect the rights of the weak, whoever objects, do it. If it be to help a powerful corporation better to serve the people, whatever the opposition, do that. Expect to be called a stand-patter, but don't be a stand-patter. Expect to be called a demagogue, but don't be a demagogue. Don't hesitate to be as revolutionary as science. Don't hesitate to be as reactionary as the multiplication table. Don't expect to build up the weak by pulling down the strong. Don't hurry to legislate. Give administration a chance to catch up with legislation. We need a broader, firmer, deeper faith in the people; a faith that men desire to do right, that the Commonwealth is founded upon a righteousness which will endure, a reconstructed faith that the final approval of the people is given not to demagogues, slavishly pandering to their selfishness, merchandising with the clamor of the hour, but to statesmen, ministering to their welfare, representing their deep, silent, abiding convictions.

Statutes must appeal to more than material welfare. Wages won't satisfy, be they never so large. Nor houses; nor lands; nor coupons, though they fall thick as the leaves of autumn.

Man has a spiritual nature. Touch it and it must respond as the magnet responds to the pole. To that, not to selfishness, let the laws of the Commonwealth appeal. Recognize the immortal worth and dignity of man. Let the laws of Massachusetts proclaim to her humblest citizen, performing the most menial task, the recognition of his manhood, the recognition that all men are peers, the humblest with the most exalted, the recognition that all work is glorified. Such is the path to equality before the law. Such is the foundation of liberty under the law. Such is the sublime revelation of man's relation to man, Democracy!

THE LIMITATIONS OF THE LAW
August 10, 1922

Vice President Coolidge addressed the American Bar Association in San Francisco in August 1922. He used the occasion to warn about the federal government's growing powers and increasing intrusions into the lives of citizens. Coolidge offered a prescient warning about what happens when citizens look to government for answers: when the laws fail to solve problems, people cry out for still more laws. As a result, Coolidge said, Americans would come to know "that type of public official who promises much, talks much, legislates much, expends much, but accomplishes little."

The growing multiplicity of laws has often been observed. The national and state legislatures pass acts, and their courts deliver opinions, which each year run into scores of thousands. A part of this is due to the increasing complexity of an advancing civilization. As new forces come into existence new relationships are created, new rights and obligations arise, which require establishment and definition by legislation and decision. These are all the natural and inevitable consequences of the growth of great cities, the development of steam and electricity, the use of the corporation as the leading factor in the transaction of business, and the attendant regulation and control of the powers created by these new and mighty agencies.

This has imposed a legal burden against which men of affairs have been wont to complain. But it is a burden which does not differ in its nature from the public requirement for security, sanitation, education, the maintenance of highways, or the other activities of government necessary to support present standards. It is all a part of the inescapable burden of existence. It follows the stream of events. It does not attempt to precede it. As human experience is broadened, it broadens with it. It represents a growth altogether natural. To resist it is to resist progress.

But there is another part of the great accumulating body of our laws that has been rapidly increasing of late, which is the result of other motives. Broadly speaking, it is the attempt to raise the moral standard of society by legislation.

The spirit of reform is altogether encouraging. The organized effort and insistent desire for an equitable distribution of the rewards of industry, for a wider justice, for a more consistent righteousness in human affairs, is one of the most stimulating and hopeful signs of the present era. There ought to be a militant public demand for progress in this direction. The society which is satisfied is lost. But in the accomplishment of these ends there needs to be a better understanding of the province of legislative and judicial action. There is danger of disappointment and disaster unless there be a wider comprehension of the limitations of the law.

The attempt to regulate, control, and prescribe all manner of conduct and social relations is very old. It was always the practice of primitive peoples. Such governments assumed jurisdiction over the action, property, life, and even religious convictions of their citizens down to the minutest detail. A large part of the history of free institutions is the history of the people struggling to emancipate themselves from all this bondage.

I do not mean by this that there has been, or can be, any progress in an attempt of the people to exist without a strong and vigorous government. That is the only foundation and the only support of all civilization. But progress has been made by the people relieving themselves of the unwarranted and unnecessary impositions of government. There exists, and must always exist, the righteous authority of the state. That is the sole source of the liberty of the individual, but it does not mean an inquisitive and officious intermeddling by attempted government action in all the affairs of the people. There is no justification for public interference with purely private concerns.

Those who founded and established the American government had a very clear understanding of this principle. They had suffered many painful experiences from too much public supervision of their private affairs. The people of that period were very jealous of all authority. It was only the statesmanship and resourcefulness of Hamilton, aided by the great influence of the wisdom and character of Washington and the sound reasoning of the very limited circle of their associates, that succeeded in proposing and adopting the American Constitution. It established a vital government of broad powers, but within distinct and prescribed limitations. Under the policy of implied powers adopted by the Federal party, its authority tended to enlarge. But under the administration of Jefferson, who, by word, though not so much by deed, questioned and resented almost all the powers of government, its authority tended to diminish, and but for the great judicial decisions of John Marshall might have become very uncertain. But while there is ground for criticism in the belittling attitude of Jefferson toward established government, there is even larger ground for approval of his policy of preserving to the people the largest possible jurisdiction and authority. After all, ours is an experiment in self-government by the people themselves, and self-government cannot be reposed wholly in some distant capital; it has to be exercised in part by the people in their own homes.

So intent were the Founding Fathers on establishing a Constitution which was confined to the fundamental principles of government that they did not turn aside even to deal with the great moral questions of slavery. That they comprehended it and regarded it as an evil was clearly demonstrated by Lincoln in his Cooper Union speech, when he showed that substantially all of them had at some time by public action made clear their opposition to the continuation of this great wrong. The early amendments were all in diminution of the power of the government and declaratory of an enlarged sovereignty of the people.

It was thus that our institutions stood for the better part of a century. There were the centralizing tendencies and the amendments arising out of the War of '61; but, while they increased to some degree the power of the national government, they were in chief great charters of liberty, confirming rights already enjoyed by the majority and undertaking to extend and guarantee like rights to those formerly deprived of equal protection of the laws. During most of this long period, the trend of public opinion and of legislation ran in the same direction. This was exemplified in the executive and legislative refusal to renew the United States Bank charter before the war and in the judicial decision in the slaughterhouse cases after the war. This decision has been both criticized and condemned in equally high places, but the result of it was perfectly clear. It was on the side of leaving to the people of the several states, and to their legislatures and courts, jurisdiction over the privileges and immunities of themselves and their own citizens.

During the past thirty years, the trend has been in the opposite direction. Urged on by the force of public opinion, national legislation has been very broadly extended for the purpose of promoting the general welfare. New powers have been delegated to the Congress by constitutional amendments, and former grants have been so interpreted as to extend legislation into new fields. This has run its course from the Interstate Commerce Act of the late eighties, through the various regulatory acts under the commerce and tax clauses, down to the maternity-aid law which recently went into effect. Much of this has been accompanied by the establishment of various commissions and boards, often clothed with much delegated power, and by providing those already in existence with new and additional authority. The national government has extended the scope of its legislation to include many kinds of regulation: the determination of traffic rates, hours of labor, wages, sumptuary laws, and into the domain of oversight of the public morals.

This has not been accomplished without what is virtually a change in the form, and actually a change in the process, of our government. The power of legislation has been to a large extent recast, for the old order looked on these increased activities with much concern. This has proceeded on the theory that it would be for the public benefit to have government to a greater degree the direct action of the people. The outcome of this doctrine has been the adoption of the direct primary, the direct election of the United States senators, the curtailment of the power of the speaker of the House, and a constant agitation for breaking down the authority of decisions of the courts. This is not the government which was put into form by Washington and Hamilton, and popularized by Jefferson. Some of the stabilizing safeguards which they had provided have been weakened. The representative element has been diminished and the democratic element has been increased, but it is still constitutional government; it still requires time, due deliberation, and the consent of the states to change or modify the fundamental law of the nation.

Advancing along this same line of centralization, of more and more legislation, of more and more power on the part of the national government, there have been proposals from time to time which would make this field almost unlimited. The authority to make laws is conferred by the very first article and section of the Constitution, but it is not general; it is limited. It is not "All legislative powers," but it is "All legislative powers herein granted shall be vested in a Congress of the United States." The purpose of that limitation was in part to prevent encroachment on the authority of the states, but more especially to safeguard and protect the liberties of the people. The men of that day proposed to be the custodians of their own freedom. In the tyrannical acts of the British Parliament, they had seen enough of a legislative body claiming to be clothed with unlimited powers.

For the purpose of protecting the people in all their rights, so dearly bought and so solemnly declared, the third article established one Supreme Court and vested it with judicial power over all cases arising under the Constitution. It is that court which has stood as the guardian and protector of our form of government, the guarantee of the perpetuity of the Constitution, and above all the great champion of the freedom and the liberty of the people. No other known tribunal has ever been devised in which the people could put their faith and confidence, to which they could intrust their choicest treasure, with a like assurance that there it would be secure and safe. There is no power, no influence, great enough to sway its judgments. There is no petitioner humble enough to be denied the full protection of its great authority. This court is human, and therefore not infallible; but in the more than one hundred and thirty years of its existence, its decisions which have not withstood the questioning of criticism could almost be counted upon one hand. In it the people have the warrant of stability, of progress, and of humanity. Wherever there is a final authority, it must be vested in mortal men. There has not been discovered a more worthy lodging place for such authority than the Supreme Court of the United States.

Such is the legislative and judicial power that the people have established in their government. Recognizing the latent forces of the Constitution, which, in accordance with the spirit of the times, have been drawn on for the purpose of promoting the public welfare, it has been very seldom that the court has been compelled to find that any humanitarian legislation was beyond the power which the people had granted to the Congress. When such a decision has been made, as in the recent case of the child-labor law, it does not mean that the court or nation wants child labor, but it simply means that the Congress has gone outside of the limitations prescribed for it by the people in their Constitution and attempted to legislate on a subject which the several states and the people themselves have chosen to keep under their own control.

Should the people desire to have the Congress pass laws relating to that over which they have not yet granted to it any jurisdiction, the way is open and plain to proceed in the same method that was taken in relation to income taxes, direct election of senators, equal suffrage, or prohibition—by an amendment to the Constitution.

One of the proposals for enlarging the present field of legislation has been to give the Congress authority to make valid a proposed law which the Supreme Court had declared was outside the authority granted by the people by the simple device of reenacting it. Such a provision would make the Congress finally supreme. In the last resort its powers practically would be unlimited. This would be to do away with the great main principle of our written Constitution, which regards the people as sovereign and the government as their agent, and would tend to make the legislative body sovereign and the people its subjects. It would to an extent substitute for the will of the people, definitely and permanently expressed in their written Constitution, the changing and uncertain will of the Congress. That would radically alter our form of government and take from it its chief guarantee of freedom.

This enlarging magnitude of legislation, these continual proposals for changes under which laws might become very excessive, whether they result from the praiseworthy motive of promoting general reform or whether they reflect the raising of the general standard of human relationship, require a new attitude on the part of the people toward their government. Our country has adopted this course. The choice has been made. It could not withdraw now if it would. But it makes it necessary to guard against the dangers which arise from this new position. It makes it necessary to keep in mind the limitation of what can be accomplished by law. It makes it necessary to adopt a new vigilance. It is not sufficient to secure legislation of this nature and leave it to go alone. It cannot execute itself. Oftentimes it will not be competently administered without the assistance of vigorous support. There must not be permitted any substitution of private will for public authority. There is required a renewed and enlarged determination to secure the observance and enforcement of the law.

So long as the national government confined itself to providing those fundamentals of liberty, order, and justice for which it was primarily established, its course was reasonably clear and plain. No large amount of revenue was required. No great swarms of public employees were necessary. There was little clash of special interests or different sections, and what there was of this nature consisted not of petty details but of broad principles. There was time for the consideration of great questions of policy. There was an opportunity for mature deliberation. What the government undertook to do it could perform with a fair degree of accuracy and precision.

But this has all been changed by embarking on a policy of a general exercise of police powers, by the public control of much private enterprise and private conduct, and of furnishing a public supply for much private need. Here are these enormous obligations which the people found they themselves were imperfectly discharging. They therefore undertook to lay their burdens on the national government. Under this weight the former accuracy of administration breaks down. The government has not at its disposal a supply of ability, honesty, and character necessary for the solution of all these problems, or an executive capacity great enough for their perfect administration. Nor is it in the possession of a wisdom which enables it to take great enterprises and manage them with no ground for criticism. We cannot rid ourselves of the human element in our affairs by an act of legislation which places them under the jurisdiction of a public commission.

The same limit of the law is manifest in the exercise of the police authority. There can be no perfect control of personal conduct by national legislation. Its attempt must be accompanied with the full expectation of very many failures. The problem of preventing vice and crime and of restraining personal and organized selfishness is as old as human experience. We shall not find for it an immediate and complete solution in an amendment to the federal Constitution, an act of Congress, or in the findings of a new board or commission. There is no magic in government not possessed by the public at large by which these things can be done. The people cannot divest themselves of their really great burdens by undertaking to provide that they shall hereafter be borne by the government.

When provision is made for far-reaching action by public authority, whether it be in the nature of an expenditure of a large sum from the Treasury or the participation in a great moral reform, it all means the imposing of large additional obligations upon the people. In the last resort it is the people who must respond. They are the military power, they are the financial power, they are the moral power of the government. There is and can be no other. When a broad rule of action is laid down by law it is they who must perform.

If this conclusion be sound it becomes necessary to avoid the danger of asking of the people more than they can do. The times are not without evidence of a deep-seated discontent not confined to any one locality or walk of life but shared in generally by those who contribute by the toil of their hand and brain to the carrying on of American enterprise. This is not the muttering of agitators; it is the conviction of the intelligence, industry, and character of the nation. There is a state of alarm, however unwarranted, on the part of many people lest they be unable to maintain themselves in their present positions. There is an apparent fear of loss of wages, loss of profits, and loss of place. There is a discernible physical and nervous exhaustion which leaves the country with little elasticity to adjust itself to the strain of events.

As the standard of civilization rises there is necessity for a larger and larger outlay to maintain the cost of existence. As the activities of government increase, as it extends its field of operations, the initial tax which it requires becomes manifolded many times when it is finally paid by the ultimate consumer.

When there is added to this aggravated financial condition an increasing amount of regulation and police control, the burden of it all becomes very great. Behind very many of these enlarging activities lies the untenable theory that there is some short cut to perfection. It is conceived that there can be a horizontal elevation of the standards of the nation, immediate and perceptible, by the simple device of new laws. This has never been the case in human experience. Progress is slow and the result of a long and arduous process of self-discipline. It is not conferred upon the people; it comes from the people. In a republic the law reflects rather than makes the standard of conduct and the state of public opinion. Real reform does not begin with a law; it ends with a law. The attempt to dragoon the body when the need is to convince the soul will end only in revolt.

Under the attempt to perform the impossible there sets in a general disintegration. When legislation fails, those who look upon it as a sovereign remedy simply cry out for more legislation. A sound and wise statesmanship which recognizes and attempts to abide by its limitations will undoubtedly find itself displaced by that type of public official who promises much, talks much, legislates much, expends much, but accomplishes little. The deliberate, sound judgment of the country is likely to find it has been superseded by a popular whim. The independence of the legislator is broken down. The enforcement of the law becomes uncertain. The courts fail in their function of speedy and accurate justice; their judgments are questioned and their independence is threatened. The law, changed and changeable on slight provocation, loses its sanctity and authority. A continuation of this condition opens the road to chaos.

These dangers must be recognized. These limits must be observed. Having embarked the government upon the enterprise of reform and regulation, it must be realized that unaided and alone it can accomplish very little. It is only one element, and that not the most powerful in the promotion of progress. When it goes into this broad field, it can furnish to the people only what the people furnish to it. Its measure of success is limited by the measure of their service.

This is very far from being a conclusion of discouragement. It is very far from being a conclusion that what legislation cannot do for the people, they cannot do for themselves. The limit of what can be done by the law is soon reached, but the limit of what can be done by an aroused and vigorous citizenship has never been exhausted. In undertaking to bear these burdens and solve these problems the government needs the continuing indulgence, cooperation, and support of the people. When the public understands that there must be an increased and increasing effort, such effort will be forthcoming. They are not ignorant of the personal equation in the administration of their affairs. When trouble arises in any quarter, they do not inquire what sort of a law they have there, but they inquire what sort of a governor and sheriff they have there. They will not long fail to observe that what kind of government they have depends upon what kind of citizens they have.

It is time to supplement the appeal to law, which is limited, with an appeal to the spirit of the people, which is unlimited. Some unsettlements disturb, but they are temporary. Some factious elements exist, but they are small. No assessment of the material conditions of Americans can warrant anything but the highest courage and the deepest faith. No reliance upon the national character has ever been betrayed. No survey which goes below the surface can fail to discover a solid and substantial foundation for satisfaction. But our countrymen must remember that they have, and can have, no dependence save themselves. Our institutions are their institutions. Our government is their government. Our laws are their laws. It is for them to enforce, support, and obey. If in this they fail, there are none who can succeed. The sanctity of duly constituted tribunals must be maintained. Undivided allegiance to public authority must be required. With a citizenship which voluntarily establishes and defends these, the cause of America is secure. Without that all else is of little avail.

DISCRIMINATING BENEVOLENCE
OCTOBER 26, 1924

This speech, delivered over the telephone to the Federation of Jewish Philanthropic Societies of New York City, demonstrates Coolidge's preoccupation with budgets and thrift. The president traces the connection between thrift and idealism, deeming a good budget "as among the noblest monuments of virtue." Coolidge emphasizes the obligation of charity to encourage individuals to improve their own lives. He commends the gathered philanthropists for fulfilling the duty of citizens to care for their communities.

When the committee representing your Federation brought me the invitation to address you this evening, I did not receive them with any very profound enthusiasm. To be confidential for a moment, I may confess that an invitation to make a speech is not the rarest experience that comes into a president's life. But I listened with, I hope, proper politeness, down to the point where your spokesman started explaining that you were to devote an evening to the consideration of a budget. Then I began to take real interest, for the budget idea, I may admit, is a sort of obsession with me. I believe in budgets. I want other people to believe in them. I have had a small one to run my own home; and besides that, I am the head of the organization that makes the greatest of all budgets, that of the United States government. Do you wonder, then, that at times I dream of balance sheets and sinking funds, and deficits, and tax rates, and all the rest?

Yes, I regard a good budget as among the noblest monuments of virtue. It is deserving of all emulation, but there are other topics that afford more obvious inspiration to popular oratory. So when I found that you actually wanted a budget speech, I felt a warming sense of gratitude. Anybody who would deliberately ask for a budget speech ought to be accommodated. I accepted the invitation, and now I want to begin by extending my hearty compliments to my audience. Your practical interest in the budget plan, your adoption of it as the basis of your great charity system, is a fine accomplishment. Wherever the same plan has been adopted, in the financing of benevolences, philanthropies, and charities through the "Community Chest" method, it has been productive of the best results. It has eliminated the waste of indiscriminate charity, but that is not by any means its most commendable accomplishment. Far more useful, I think, is the service it has done in organizing these works of human helpfulness so that we may be sure they will not do more harm than good. Nothing is finer than the open hand and the generous heart that prompts free and unselfish giving. But modern social science knows, also, that ill-directed charity is often directly responsible for encouragement of pauperism and mendicancy. The best service we can do for the needy and the unfortunate is to help them in such manner that their self respect, their ability to help themselves, shall not be injured but augmented. Nobody is necessarily out merely because he is down. But, being down, nobody gets up again without honest effort of his own. The best help that benevolence and philanthropy can give is that which induces everybody to help himself.

Your Federation for the Support of Jewish Philanthropic Societies in New York is the central financial agency, I am told, for no less than ninety-one various philanthropies, which receive annual support aggregating $7,000,000. Among them are hospitals, orphanages, a great relief society, a loaning organization, a home for aged and infirm. The Young Men's Hebrew Association and the Young Women's Hebrew Association do social and educational work of the greatest value. Especial attention is devoted indeed to educational effort for which technical schools are maintained. That is, of course, precisely what we should expect from a great Jewish organization, for the Jews are always among the first to appreciate and to utilize educational opportunities.

Into this entire system of communal services, reaching to every possible department of social relations, the Federation brings order and a proper interrelationship. Duplication of services, which always means multiplication of expense and division of results, is avoided. The man or woman who gives through this agency, knows that the most good will be done at the least expense. All administrative costs of the organization have averaged less than four cents on the dollar. Other "Community Chest" activities, which in recent years are getting spread all about the country, make like showings of efficiency and economical management. They have been able, just as your Federation has been able, to enlist the best abilities, the most skilled direction, the widest experience, in systematizing operations that ordinarily are haphazard and wasteful.

But, with all of my regard for the strictly business aspect of this splendid modern program, I must emphasize once more that to me the greatest good of these communal organizations of benevolence lies in their immeasurably greater capacity for real good. There is an impressive array of testimony that the

average dollar of indiscriminate, well-meaning, ignorant dona-
tion to charity is mostly wasted. Many such dollars are far worse
than wasted. You seek no cold and heartless elimination of sentiment from your charitable works. You have, however, sought
to substitute sense for sentimentality, and that is altogether to
be desired.

The Jewish people have always and everywhere been particularly devoted to the ideal of taking care of their own. This
Federation is one of the monuments to their independence and
self-reliance. They have sought to protect and preserve that
wonderful inheritance of tradition, culture, literature, and religion which has placed the world under so many obligations to
them. In their efforts to serve their own highest ideals, they
will always be helpful to the wider community of which they
are a part. In the work of this Federation, they are rendering
a service not only to their own people but to the entire community. Along with that precious service, they are setting up an
example of successful, practical, helpful business administration
which deserves all commendation. It may well be an inspiration
to every charitable agency in the land.

I want you to know that I feel you are making good citizens, that you are strengthening the government, that you are
demonstrating the supremacy of the spiritual life and helping
establish the Kingdom of God on earth.

INAUGURAL ADDRESS
March 4, 1925

*Coolidge triumphed in the 1924 election, earning an absolute majority
of votes in a three-candidate race. His inaugural address in 1925 was
the first such address to be carried nationally by radio. The speech's*

audio suffered from some technical complications that created an echo, but its content clearly articulated Coolidge's governing philosophy. The president made a point of emphasizing the continued importance of government thrift, saying, "I favor the policy of economy, not because I wish to save money, but because I wish to save people."

No one can contemplate current conditions without finding much that is satisfying and still more that is encouraging. Our own country is leading the world in the general readjustment to the results of the great conflict. Many of its burdens will bear heavily upon us for years, and the secondary and indirect effects we must expect to experience for some time. But we are beginning to comprehend more definitely what course should be pursued, what remedies ought to be applied, what actions should be taken for our deliverance, and are clearly manifesting a determined will faithfully and conscientiously to adopt these methods of relief.

Already we have sufficiently rearranged our domestic affairs so that confidence has returned, business has revived, and we appear to be entering an era of prosperity which is gradually reaching into every part of the nation. Realizing that we cannot live unto ourselves alone, we have contributed of our resources and our counsel to the relief of the suffering and the settlement of the disputes among the European nations. Because of what America is and what America has done, a firmer courage, a higher hope, inspires the heart of all humanity.

These results have not occurred by mere chance. They have been secured by a constant and enlightened effort marked by many sacrifices and extending over many generations. We cannot continue these brilliant successes in the future unless we continue to learn from the past. It is necessary to keep the former experiences of our country both at home and abroad continually before us if we are to have any science of government.

If we wish to erect new structures, we must have a definite knowledge of the old foundations. We must realize that human nature is about the most constant thing in the universe and that the essentials of human relationship do not change. We must frequently take our bearings from these fixed stars of our political firmament if we expect to hold a true course. If we examine carefully what we have done, we can determine the more accurately what we can do.

We stand at the opening of the one hundred and fiftieth year since our national consciousness first asserted itself by unmistakable action with an array of force. The old sentiment of detached and dependent colonies disappeared in the new sentiment of a united and independent nation. Men began to discard the narrow confines of a local charter for the broader opportunities of a national constitution. Under the eternal urge of freedom, we became an independent nation. A little less than fifty years later, that freedom and independence were reasserted in the face of all the world, and guarded, supported, and secured by the Monroe Doctrine.

The narrow fringe of states along the Atlantic seaboard advanced its frontiers across the hills and plains of an intervening continent until it passed down the golden slope to the Pacific. We made freedom a birthright. We extended our domain over distant islands in order to safeguard our own interests and accepted the consequent obligation to bestow justice and liberty upon less-favored peoples. In the defense of our own ideals and in the general cause of liberty, we entered the Great War. When victory had been fully secured, we withdrew to our own shores unrecompensed save in the consciousness of duty done.

Throughout all these experiences, we have enlarged our freedom, we have strengthened our independence. We have been, and propose to be, more and more American. We believe that we can best serve our own country and most successfully discharge our obligations to humanity by continuing to be openly and candidly, intensely and scrupulously, American. If we have any heritage, it has been that. If we have any destiny, we have found it in that direction.

But if we wish to continue to be distinctively American, we must continue to make that term comprehensive enough to embrace the legitimate desires of a civilized and enlightened people determined in all their relations to pursue a conscientious and religious life. We cannot permit ourselves to be narrowed and dwarfed by slogans and phrases. It is not the adjective, but the substantive, which is of real importance. It is not the name of the action, but the result of the action, which is the chief concern. It will be well not to be too much disturbed by the thought of either isolation or entanglement of pacifists and militarists. The physical configuration of the earth has separated us from all of the Old World, but the common brotherhood of man, the highest law of all our being, has united us by inseparable bonds with all humanity. Our country represents nothing but peaceful intentions toward all the earth, but it ought not to fail to maintain such a military force as comports with the dignity and security of a great people. It ought to be a balanced force, intensely modern, capable of defense by sea and land, beneath the surface and in the air. But it should be so conducted that all the world may see in it, not a menace, but an instrument of security and peace.

This nation believes thoroughly in an honorable peace under which the rights of its citizens are to be everywhere protected. It has never found that the necessary enjoyment of such a peace could be maintained only by a great and threatening array of arms. In common with other nations, it is now more determined than ever to promote peace through friendliness

and good will, through mutual understandings and mutual forbearance. We have never practiced the policy of competitive
armaments. We have recently committed ourselves by covenants
with the other great nations to a limitation of our sea power.
As one result of this, our Navy ranks larger, in comparison,
than it ever did before. Removing the burden of expense and
jealousy, which must always accrue from a keen rivalry, is one
of the most effective methods of diminishing that unreasonable
hysteria and misunderstanding which are the most potent means
of fomenting war. This policy represents a new departure in the
world. It is a thought, an ideal, which has led to an entirely new
line of action. It will not be easy to maintain. Some never move
from their old position, some are constantly slipping back to the
old ways of thought and the old action of seizing a musket and
relying on force. America has taken the lead in this new direction, and that lead America must continue to hold. If we expect
others to rely on our fairness and justice we must show that we
rely on their fairness and justice.

If we are to judge by past experience, there is much to be
hoped for in international relations from frequent conferences
and consultations. We have before us the beneficial results
of the Washington conference and the various consultations
recently held upon European affairs, some of which were in
response to our suggestions and in some of which we were
active participants. Even the failures cannot but be accounted
useful and an immeasurable advance over threatened or actual
warfare. I am strongly in favor of continuation of this policy,
whenever conditions are such that there is even a promise that
practical and favorable results might be secured.

In conformity with the principle that a display of reason
rather than a threat of force should be the determining factor in the intercourse among nations, we have long advocated

the peaceful settlement of disputes by methods of arbitration
and have negotiated many treaties to secure that result. The
same considerations should lead to our adherence to the Permanent Court of International Justice. Where great principles are
involved, where great movements are under way which promise
much for the welfare of humanity by reason of the very fact
that many other nations have given such movements their actual
support, we ought not to withhold our own sanction because of
any small and inessential difference, but only upon the ground
of the most important and compelling fundamental reasons. We
cannot barter away our independence or our sovereignty, but
we ought to engage in no refinements of logic, no sophistries,
and no subterfuges to argue away the undoubted duty of this
country by reason of the might of its numbers, the power of its
resources, and its position of leadership in the world, actively and
comprehensively to signify its approval and to bear its full share
of their responsibility of a candid and disinterested attempt at
the establishment of a tribunal for the administration of even-
handed justice between nation and nation. The weight of our
enormous influence must be cast upon the side of a reign not of
force but of law and trial, not by battle but by reason.

We have never any wish to interfere in the political conditions of any other countries. Especially are we determined not
to become implicated in the political controversies of the Old
World. With a great deal of hesitation, we have responded to
appeals for help to maintain order, protect life and property, and
establish responsible government in some of the small countries
of the Western Hemisphere. Our private citizens have advanced
large sums of money to assist in the necessary financing and
relief of the Old World. We have not failed, nor shall we fail to
respond, whenever necessary to mitigate human suffering and
assist in the rehabilitation of distressed nations. These, too, are

requirements which must be met by reason of our vast powers and the place we hold in the world.

Some of the best thought of mankind has long been seeking for a formula for permanent peace. Undoubtedly the clarification of the principles of international law would be helpful, and the efforts of scholars to prepare such a work for adoption by the various nations should have our sympathy and support. Much may be hoped for from the earnest studies of those who advocate the outlawing of aggressive war. But all these plans and preparations, these treaties and covenants, will not of themselves be adequate. One of the greatest dangers to peace lies in the economic pressure to which people find themselves subjected. One of the most practical things to be done in the world is to seek arrangements under which such pressure may be removed so that opportunity may be renewed and hope may be revived. There must be some assurance that effort and endeavor will be followed by success and prosperity. In the making and financing of such adjustments there is not only an opportunity but a real duty for America to respond with her counsel and her resources. Conditions must be provided under which people can make a living and work out of their difficulties. But there is another element, more important than all, without which there cannot be the slightest hope of a permanent peace. That element lies in the heart of humanity. Unless the desire for peace be cherished there, unless this fundamental and only natural source of brotherly love be cultivated to its highest degree, all artificial efforts will be in vain. Peace will come when there is realization that only under a reign of law, based on righteousness and supported by the religious conviction of the brotherhood of man, can there be any hope of a complete and satisfying life. Parchment will fail, the sword will fail, it is only the spiritual nature of man that can be triumphant.

It seems altogether probable that we can contribute most to these important objects by maintaining our position of political detachment and independence. We are not identified with any Old World interests. This position should be made more and more clear in our relations with all foreign countries. We are at peace with all of them. Our program is never to oppress, but always to assist. But while we do justice to others, we must require that justice be done to us. With us a treaty of peace means peace, and a treaty of amity means amity. We have made great contributions to the settlement of contentious differences in both Europe and Asia. But there is a very definite point beyond which we cannot go. We can only help those who help themselves. Mindful of these limitations, the one great duty that stands out requires us to use our enormous powers to trim the balance of the world.

While we can look with a great deal of pleasure upon what we have done abroad, we must remember that our continued success in that direction depends upon what we do at home. Since its very outset, it has been found necessary to conduct our government by means of political parties. That system would not have survived from generation to generation if it had not been fundamentally sound and provided the best instrumentalities for the most complete expression of the popular will. It is not necessary to claim that it has always worked perfectly. It is enough to know that nothing better has been devised. No one would deny that there should be full and free expression and an opportunity for independence of action within the party. There is no salvation in a narrow and bigoted partisanship. But if there is to be responsible party government, the party label must be something more than a mere device for securing office. Unless those who are elected under the same party designation are willing to assume sufficient responsibility and exhibit sufficient loyalty and coherence so that they can cooperate with each other in the support of the broad general principles of the party platform, the election is merely a mockery, no decision is made at the polls, and there is no representation of the popular will. Common honesty and good faith with the people who support a party at the polls require that party, when it enters office, to assume the control of that portion of the government to which it has been elected. Any other course is bad faith and a violation of the party pledges.

When the country has bestowed its confidence upon a party by making it a majority in the Congress, it has a right to expect such unity of action as will make the party majority an effective instrument of government. This administration has come into power with a very clear and definite mandate from the people. The expression of the popular will in favor of maintaining our constitutional guarantees was overwhelming and decisive. There was a manifestation of such faith in the integrity of the courts that we can consider that issue rejected for some time to come. Likewise, the policy of public ownership of railroads and certain electric utilities met with unmistakable defeat. The people declared that they wanted their rights to have not a political but a judicial determination, and their independence and freedom continued and supported by having the ownership and control of their property, not in the government, but in their own hands. As they always do when they have a fair chance, the people demonstrated that they are sound and are determined to have a sound government.

When we turn from what was rejected to inquire what was accepted, the policy that stands out with the greatest clearness is that of economy in public expenditure with reduction and reform of taxation. The principle involved in this effort is that of conservation. The resources of this country are almost beyond computation. No mind can comprehend them. But the cost of our combined governments is likewise almost beyond definition. Not only those who are now making their tax returns, but those who meet the enhanced cost of existence in their monthly bills, know by hard experience what this great burden is and what it does. No matter what others may want, these people want a drastic economy. They are opposed to waste. They know that extravagance lengthens the hours and diminishes the rewards of their labor. I favor the policy of economy, not because I wish to save money, but because I wish to save people. The men and women of this country who toil are the ones who bear the cost of the government. Every dollar that we carelessly waste means that their life will be so much the more meager. Every dollar that we prudently save means that their life will be so much the more abundant. Economy is idealism in its most practical form.

If extravagance were not reflected in taxation, and through taxation both directly and indirectly injuriously affecting the people, it would not be of so much consequence. The wisest and soundest method of solving our tax problem is through economy. Fortunately, of all the great nations this country is best in a position to adopt that simple remedy. We do not any longer need wartime revenues. The collection of any taxes which are not absolutely required, which do not beyond reasonable doubt contribute to the public welfare, is only a species of legalized larceny. Under this republic, the rewards of industry belong to those who earn them. The only constitutional tax is the tax which ministers to public necessity. The property of the country belongs to the people of the country. Their title is absolute. They do not support any privileged class; they do not need to maintain great military forces; they ought not to be burdened with a great array of public employees. They are not required to make any contribution to government expenditures except that which they voluntarily assess upon themselves through the action of their own representatives. Whenever taxes become burdensome, a remedy can be applied by the people; but if they do not act for themselves, no one can be very successful in acting for them.

The time is arriving when we can have further tax reduction, when, unless we wish to hamper the people in their right to earn a living, we must have tax reform. The method of raising revenue ought not to impede the transaction of business; it ought to encourage it. I am opposed to extremely high rates because they produce little or no revenue, because they are bad for the country, and, finally, because they are wrong. We cannot finance the country, we cannot improve social conditions, through any system of injustice, even if we attempt to inflict it upon the rich. Those who suffer the most harm will be the poor. This country believes in prosperity. It is absurd to suppose that it is envious of those who are already prosperous. The wise and correct course to follow in taxation and all other economic legislation is not to destroy those who have already secured success but to create conditions under which everyone will have a better chance to be successful. The verdict of the country has been given on this question. That verdict stands. We shall do well to heed it.

These questions involve moral issues. We need not concern ourselves much about the rights of property if we will faithfully observe the rights of persons. Under our institutions, their rights are supreme. It is not property but the right to hold property, both great and small, which our Constitution guarantees. All owners of property are charged with a service. These rights and duties have been revealed, through the conscience of society, to have a divine sanction. The very stability of our society rests upon production and conservation. For individuals or for governments to waste and squander their resources is to deny these rights and disregard these obligations. The result of economic dissipation to a nation is always moral decay.

These policies of better international understandings, greater economy, and lower taxes have contributed largely to peaceful and prosperous industrial relations. Under the helpful influences of restrictive immigration and a protective tariff, employment is plentiful, the rate of pay is high, and wage earners are in a state of contentment seldom before seen. Our transportation systems have been gradually recovering and have been able to meet all the requirements of the service. Agriculture has been very slow in reviving, but the price of cereals at last indicates that the day of its deliverance is at hand.

We are not without our problems, but our most important problem is not to secure new advantages but to maintain those which we already possess. Our system of government made up of three separate and independent departments, our divided sovereignty composed of nation and state, the matchless wisdom that is enshrined in our Constitution, all these need constant effort and tireless vigilance for their protection and support.

In a republic, the first rule for the guidance of the citizen is obedience to law. Under a despotism, the law may be imposed upon the subject. He has no voice in its making, no influence in its administration, it does not represent him. Under a free government, the citizen makes his own laws, chooses his own administrators, which do represent him. Those who want their rights respected under the Constitution and the law ought to set the example themselves of observing the Constitution and the law. While there may be those of high intelligence who violate the law at times, the barbarian and the defective always violate it. Those who disregard the rules of society are not exhibiting a superior intelligence, are not promoting freedom and independence, are not following the path of civilization, but are displaying the traits of ignorance, of servitude, of savagery, and treading the way that leads back to the jungle.

The essence of a republic is representative government. Our Congress represents the people and the states. In all legislative affairs it is the natural collaborator with the President. In spite of all the criticism which often falls to its lot, I do not hesitate to say that there is no more independent and effective legislative body in the world. It is, and should be, jealous of its prerogative. I welcome its cooperation and expect to share with it not only the responsibility but the credit for our common effort to secure beneficial legislation.

These are some of the principles which America represents. We have not by any means put them fully into practice, but we have strongly signified our belief in them. The encouraging feature of our country is not that it has reached its destination, but that it has overwhelmingly expressed its determination to proceed in the right direction. It is true that we could, with profit, be less sectional and more national in our thought. It would be well if we could replace much that is only a false and ignorant prejudice with a true and enlightened pride of race. But the last election showed that appeals to class and nationality had little effect. We were all found loyal to a common citizenship. The fundamental precept of liberty is toleration. We cannot permit any inquisition either within or without the law or apply any religious test to the holding of office. The mind of America must be forever free.

It is in such contemplations, my fellow countrymen, which are not exhaustive but only representative, that I find ample warrant for satisfaction and encouragement. We should not let the much that is to do obscure the much which has been done. The past and present show faith and hope and courage fully justified. Here stands our country, an example of tranquility at home, a patron of tranquility abroad. Here stands its government, aware of its might but obedient to its conscience. Here it will continue to stand, seeking peace and prosperity, solicitous for the welfare of the wage earner, promoting enterprise, developing waterways and natural resources, attentive to the intuitive counsel of womanhood, encouraging education, desiring the advancement of religion, supporting the cause of justice and honor among the nations. America seeks no earthly empire built on blood and force. No ambition, no temptation, lures her to thought of foreign dominions. The legions which she sends forth are armed, not with the sword, but with the cross. The higher state to which she seeks the allegiance of all mankind is not of human but of divine origin. She cherishes no purpose save to merit the favor of Almighty God.

TOLERATION AND LIBERALISM
OCTOBER 6, 1925

President Coolidge traveled to Omaha, Nebraska, in October 1925 to address the American Legion Convention. He spoke at a time of increasing racial and ethnic tensions: tens of thousands of Ku Klux Klan members had marched on Washington that summer, and a wave of anti-immigrant sentiment had led to passage of the Immigration Act the previous year. Coolidge had signed the act, but not because he was anti-immigrant. Rather, he believed that the United States needed time to settle down after World War I to be able to absorb more immigrants in the future.

Here Coolidge explains his perspective on the world. He calls for tolerance, which he defines as "respect for different kinds of good." The president also makes clear his opposition to discrimination against immigrants.

It is a high privilege to sit as a member of this convention. Those who exercise it have been raised to the rank of a true nobility. It is a mark of personal merit which did not come by right of birth but by right of conquest. No one can ever question your title as patriots. No one can ever doubt the place of affection and honor which you hold forevermore in the heart of the nation. Your right to be here results from what you dared and what you did and the sacrifices which you made for our common country. It is all a glorious story of American enterprise and American valor.

The magnitude of the service which you rendered to your country and to humanity is beyond estimation. Sharp outlines here and there we know, but the whole account of the World War would be on a scale so stupendous that it could never be recorded. In the victory which was finally gained by you and your foreign comrades, you represented on the battlefield the united efforts of our whole people. You were there as the result of a great resurgence of the old American spirit, which manifested itself in a thousand ways, by the pouring out of vast sums of money in credits and charities, by the organization and quickening of every hand in our extended industries, by the expansion of agriculture until it met the demands of famishing continents, by the manufacture of an unending stream of munitions and supplies, by the creation of vast fleets of war and transport ships, and, finally, when the tide of battle was turning against our associates, by bringing into action a great armed force on sea and land of a character that the world had never seen before, which, when it finally took its place in the line, never ceased to advance, carrying the cause of liberty to a triumphant conclusion. You reaffirmed the position of this nation in the estimation of mankind. You saved civilization from a gigantic reverse. Nobody says now that Americans cannot fight.

Our people were influenced by many motives to undertake
to carry on this gigantic conflict, but we went in and came out
singularly free from those questionable causes and results which
have often characterized other wars. We were not moved by the
age-old antagonisms of racial jealousies and hatreds. We were
not seeking to gratify the ambitions of any reigning dynasty.
We were not inspired by trade and commercial rivalries. We
harbored no imperialistic designs. We feared no other country.
We coveted no territory. But the time came when we were
compelled to defend our own property and protect the rights
and lives of our own citizens. We believed, moreover, that those
institutions which we cherish with a supreme affection, and
which lie at the foundation of our whole scheme of human relationship, the right of freedom, of equality, of self-government,
were all in jeopardy. We thought the question was involved
of whether the people of the earth were to rule or whether
they were to be ruled. We thought that we were helping to
determine whether the principle of despotism or the principle
of liberty should be the prevailing standard among the nations.
Then, too, our country all came under the influence of a great
wave of idealism. The crusading spirit was aroused. The cause
of civilization, the cause of humanity, made a compelling appeal.
No doubt there were other motives, but these appear to me the
chief causes which drew America into the World War.

In a conflict which engaged all the major nations of the
earth and lasted for a period exceeding four years, there could
be no expectation of material gains. War in its very essence
means destruction. Never before were contending peoples so
well equipped with every kind of infernal engine calculated to
spread desolation on land and over the face of the deep. Our
country is only but now righting itself and beginning a moderate but steady recovery from the great economic loss which it

sustained. That tremendous debt must be liquidated through the laborious toil of our people. Modern warfare becomes more and more to mean utter loss, destruction, and desolation of the best that there is of any people, its valiant youth and its accumulated treasure. If our country secured any benefit, if it met with any gain, it must have been in moral and spiritual values. It must be not because it made its fortune but because it found its soul. Others may disagree with me, but in spite of some incidental and trifling difficulties it is my firm opinion that America has come out of the war with a stronger determination to live by the rule of righteousness and pursue the course of truth and justice in both our domestic and foreign relations. No one can deny that we have protected the rights of our citizens, laid a firmer foundation for our institutions of liberty, and made our contribution to the cause of civilization and humanity. In doing all this we found that, though of many different nationalities, our people had a spiritual bond. They were all Americans.

When we look over the rest of the world, in spite of all its devastation there is encouragement to believe it is on a firmer moral foundation than it was in 1914. Much of the old despotism has been swept away. While some of it comes creeping back disguised under new names, no one can doubt that the general admission of the right of the people to self-government has made tremendous progress in nearly every quarter of the globe. In spite of the staggering losses and the grievous burden of taxation, there is a new note of hope for the individual to be more secure in his rights, which is unmistakably clearer than ever before. With all the troubles that beset the Old World, the former cloud of fear is evidently not now so appalling. It is impossible to believe that any nation now feels that it could better itself by war, and it is apparent to me that there has been a very distinct advance in the policy of peaceful and honorable adjustment of international differences. War has become less probable; peace has become more secure. The price which has been paid to bring about this new condition is utterly beyond comprehension. We cannot see why it should not have come in orderly and peaceful methods without the attendant shock of fire and sword and carnage. We only know that it is here. We believe that on the ruins of the old order a better civilization is being constructed.

We had our domestic problems which resulted from the war. The chief of these was the care and relief of the afflicted veterans and their dependents. This was a tremendous task, on which about $3 billion has already been expended. No doubt there have been cases where the unworthy have secured aid, while the worthy have gone unrelieved. Some mistakes were inevitable, but our people and our government have at all times been especially solicitous to discharge most faithfully this prime obligation. What is now being done is related to you in detail by General Hines, of the Veterans' Bureau, a public official of demonstrated merit, so that I shall not dwell upon it. During the past year, under the distinguished and efficient leadership of Commander Drain, the Legion itself has undertaken to provide an endowment fund of $5 million to minister to the charitable requirements of their comrades. The response to this appeal has been most generous and the results appear most promising. The government can do much, but it can never supply the personal relationship that comes from the ministrations of a private charity of that kind.

The next most pressing problem was the better ordering of the finances of the nation. Our government was costing almost more than it was worth. It had more people on the payroll than were necessary, all of which made expenses too much and taxes too high. This inflated condition contributed to the depression which began in 1920. But the government expenditures have been almost cut in two, taxes have been twice reduced, and the incoming Congress will provide further reductions. Deflation has run its course and an era of business activity and general prosperity, exceeding anything ever before experienced in this country and fairly well distributed among all our people, is already at hand.

Our country has a larger Army and a more powerful Navy, costing annually almost twice as much as it ever before had in time of peace. I am a thorough believer in a policy of adequate military preparation. We are constantly working to perfect our defenses in every branch, land forces, air forces, surface and submarine forces. That work will continue. Our military establishment of the Army and Navy, the National Guard, and the Reserve Corps is far superior to anything we have ever maintained before, except in time of war. In the past six years we have expended about $4 billion for this purpose. That ought to show results, and those who have correct information know that it does show results. The country can rest assured that if security lies in military force, it was never so secure before in all its history.

We have been attempting to relieve ourselves and the other nations from the old theory of competitive armaments. In spite of all the arguments in favor of great military forces, no nation ever had an army large enough to guarantee it against attack in time of peace or to insure its victory in time of war. No nation ever will. Peace and security are more likely to result from fair and honorable dealings, and mutual agreements for a limitation of armaments among nations, than by any attempt at competition in squadrons and battalions. No doubt this country could, if it wished to spend more money, make a better military force, but that is only part of the problem which confronts our government. The real question is whether spending more money to make a better military force would really make a better country. I would be the last to disparage the military art. It is an honorable and patriotic calling of the highest rank. But I can see no merit in any unnecessary expenditure of money to hire men to build fleets and carry muskets when international relations and agreements permit the turning of such resources into the making of good roads, the building of better homes, the promotion of education, and all the other arts of peace which minister to the advancement of human welfare. Happily, the position of our country is such among the other nations of the world that we have been and shall be warranted in proceeding in this direction.

While it is true that we are paying out far more money and maintaining a much stronger military establishment than ever before because of the conditions stated, we have been able to pursue a moderate course. Our people have had all the war, all the taxation, and all the military service that they want. They have therefore wished to emphasize their attachment to our ancient policy of peace. They have insisted upon economy. They have supported the principle of limitation of armaments. They have been able to do this because of their position and their strength in numbers and in resources. We have a tremendous natural power which supplements our arms. We are conscious that no other nation harbors any design to put us in jeopardy.

It is our purpose in our intercourse with foreign powers to rely not on the strength of our fleets and our armies but on the justice of our cause. For these reasons our country has not wished to maintain huge military forces. It has been convinced that it could better serve itself and better serve humanity by using its resources for other purposes.

In dealing with our military problems, there is one principle that is exceedingly important. Our institutions are founded not on military power but on civil authority. We are irrevocably committed to the theory of a government by the people. We have our constitutions and our laws, our executives, our legislatures, and our courts, but ultimately we are governed by public opinion. Our forefathers had seen so much of militarism, and suffered so much from it, that they desired to banish it forever. They believed and declared in at least one of their state constitutions that the military power should be subordinate to and governed by the civil authority. It is for this reason that any organization of men in the military service bent on inflaming the public mind for the purpose of forcing government action through the pressure of public opinion is an exceedingly dangerous undertaking and precedent. This is so whatever form it might take, whether it be for the purpose of influencing the executive, the legislature, or the heads of departments. It is for the civil authority to determine what appropriations shall be granted, what appointments shall be made, and what rules shall be adopted for the conduct of its armed forces. Whenever the military power starts dictating to the civil authority, by whatsoever means adopted, the liberties of the country are beginning to end. National defense should at all times be supported, but any form of militarism should be resisted.

Undoubtedly one of the most important provisions in the preparation for national defense is a proper and sound selective service act. Such a law ought to give authority for a very broad mobilization of all the resources of the country, both persons and materials. I can see some difficulties in the application of the principle, for it is the payment of a higher price that stimulates an increased production, but whenever it can be done without economic dislocation, such limits ought to be established in time of war as would prevent so far as possible all kinds of profiteering. There is little defense which can be made of a system which puts some men in the ranks on very small pay and leaves others undisturbed to reap very large profits. Even the income tax, which recaptured for the benefit of the national Treasury alone about 75 percent of such profits, while local governments took part of the remainder, is not a complete answer. The laying of taxes is, of course, in itself a conscription of whatever is necessary of the wealth of the country for national defense, but taxation does not meet the full requirements of the situation. In the advent of war, power should be lodged somewhere for the stabilization of prices as far as that might be possible in justice to the country and its defenders.

But it will always be impossible to harmonize justice and war. It is always possible to purchase materials with money, but patriotism cannot be purchased. Unless the people are willing to defend their country because of their belief in it, because of their affection for it, and because it is representative of their home, their country cannot be defended. If we are looking for a more complete reign of justice, a more complete supremacy of law, a more complete social harmony, we must seek it in the paths of peace. Progress in these directions under the present order of the world is not likely to be made except during a state of domestic and international tranquility. One of the great questions before the nations today is how to promote such tranquility.

The economic problems of society are important. On the whole, we are meeting them fairly well. They are so personal and so pressing that they never fail to receive constant attention. But they are only a part. We need to put a proper emphasis on the other problems of society. We need to consider what attitude of the public mind it is necessary to cultivate in order that a mixed population like our own may dwell together more harmoniously and the family of nations reach a better state of understanding. You who have been in the service know how absolutely necessary it is in a military organization that the individual subordinate some part of his personality for the general good. That is the one great lesson which results from the training of a soldier. Whoever has been taught that lesson in camp and field is thereafter the better equipped to appreciate that it is equally applicable in other departments of life. It is necessary in the home, in industry and commerce, in scientific and intellectual development. At the foundation of every strong and mature character we find this trait which is best described as being subject to discipline. The essence of it is toleration. It is toleration in the broadest and most inclusive sense, a liberality of mind, which gives to the opinions and judgments of others the same generous consideration that it asks for its own, and which is moved by the spirit of the philosopher who declared that "To know all is to forgive all." It may not be given to infinite beings to attain that ideal, but it is none the less one toward which we should strive.

One of the most natural of reactions during the war was intolerance. But the inevitable disregard for the opinions and feelings of minorities is nonetheless a disturbing product of war psychology. The slow and difficult advances which tolerance and liberalism have made through long periods of development are dissipated almost in a night when the necessary wartime habits of thought hold the minds of the people. The necessity for a common purpose and a united intellectual front becomes paramount to everything else. But when the need for such a solidarity is past, there should be a quick and generous readiness to revert to the old and normal habits of thought. There should be an intellectual demobilization as well as a military demobilization. Progress depends very largely on the encouragement of variety. Whatever tends to standardize the community, to establish fixed and rigid modes of thought, tends to fossilize society. If we all believed the same thing and thought the same thoughts and applied the same valuations to all the occurrences about us, we should reach a state of equilibrium closely akin to an intellectual and spiritual paralysis. It is the ferment of ideas, the clash of disagreeing judgments, the privilege of the individual to develop his own thoughts and shape his own character, that makes progress possible. It is not possible to learn much from those who uniformly agree with us. But many useful things are learned from those who disagree with us; and even when we can gain nothing, our differences are likely to do us no harm.

In this period of after-war rigidity, suspicion, and intolerance, our own country has not been exempt from unfortunate experiences. Thanks to our comparative isolation, we have known less of the international frictions and rivalries than some other countries less fortunately situated. But among some of the varying racial, religious, and social groups of our people, there have been manifestations of an intolerance of opinion, a narrowness to outlook, a fixity of judgment, against which we may well be warned. It is not easy to conceive of anything that would be more unfortunate in a community based upon the ideals of which Americans boast than any considerable development of intolerance as regards religion. To a great extent this country owes its beginnings to the determination of our hardy ancestors to maintain complete freedom in religion. Instead of a state church, we have decreed that every citizen shall be free to follow the dictates of his own conscience as to his religious beliefs and affiliations. Under that guarantee we have erected a system which certainly is justified by its fruits. Under no other could we have dared to invite the peoples of all countries and creeds to come here and unite with us in creating the state of which we are all citizens.

But having invited them here, having accepted their great and varied contributions to the building of the nation, it is for us to maintain in all good faith those liberal institutions and traditions which have been so productive of good.

The bringing together of all these different national, racial, religious, and cultural elements has made our country a kind of composite of the rest of the world, and we can render no greater service than by demonstrating the possibility of harmonious cooperation among so many various groups. Every one of them has something characteristic and significant of great value to cast into the common fund of our material, intellectual, and spiritual resources. The war brought a great test of our experiment in amalgamating these varied factors into a real nation, with the ideals and aspirations of a united people. None was excepted from the obligation to serve when the hour of danger struck. The event proved that our theory had been sound. On a solid foundation of a national unity there had been erected a super-structure which in its varied parts had offered full opportunity to develop all the range of talents and genius that had gone into its making. Well-nigh all the races, religions, and nationalities of the world were represented in the armed forces of this nation, as they were in the body of our population. No man's patriotism was impugned or service questioned because of his racial origin, his political opinion, or his religious convictions. Immigrants and sons of immigrants from the central European countries fought side by side with those who descended from the countries which were our allies; with the sons of equatorial Africa; and with the Red men of our own aboriginal population, all of them equally proud of the name Americans.

We must not, in times of peace, permit ourselves to lose any part from this structure of patriotic unity. I make no plea for leniency toward those who are criminal or vicious, are open enemies of society and are not prepared to accept the true standards of our citizenship. By tolerance I do not mean indifference to evil. I mean respect for different kinds of good. Whether one traces his Americanism back three centuries to the *Mayflower*, or three years to the steerage, is not half so important as whether his Americanism of today is real and genuine. No matter by what various crafts we came here, we are all now in the same boat. You men constituted the crew of our "Ship of State" during her passage through the roughest waters. You made up the watch and held the danger posts when the storm was fiercest. You brought her safely and triumphantly into port. Out of that experience you have learned the lessons of discipline, tolerance, respect for authority, and regard for the basic manhood of your neighbor. You bore aloft a standard of patriotic conduct and civic integrity to which all could repair. Such a standard, with a like common appeal, must be upheld just as firmly and unitedly now in time of peace. Among citizens honestly devoted to the maintenance of that standard, there need be small concern about differences of individual opinion in other regards. Granting first the essentials of loyalty to our country and to our fundamental institutions, we may not only overlook, but we may encourage, differences of opinion as to other things. For differences of this kind will certainly be elements of strength rather than of weakness. They will give variety to our tastes and interests. They will broaden our vision, strengthen our understanding, encourage the true humanities, and enrich our whole mode and conception of life. I recognize the full and complete necessity of 100 percent Americanism, but 100 percent Americanism may be made up of many various elements.

If we are to have that harmony and tranquility, that union of spirit which is the foundation of real national genius and national progress, we must all realize that there are true

Americans who did not happen to be born in our section of the country, who do not attend our place of religious worship, who are not of our racial stock, or who are not proficient in our language. If we are to create on this continent a free republic and an enlightened civilization that will be capable of reflecting the true greatness and glory of mankind, it will be necessary to regard these differences as accidental and unessential. We shall have to look beyond the outward manifestations of race and creed. Divine Providence has not bestowed upon any race a monopoly of patriotism and character.

The same principle that it is necessary to apply to the attitude of mind among our own people it is also necessary to apply to the attitude of mind among the different nations. During the war we were required not only to put a strong emphasis on everything that appealed to our own national pride but an equally strong emphasis on that which tended to disparage other peoples. There was an intensive cultivation of animosities and hatreds and enmities, together with a blind appeal to force, that took possession of substantially all the peoples of the earth. Of course, these ministered to the war spirit. They supplied the incentive for destruction, the motive for conquest. But in time of peace these sentiments are not helps but hindrances; they are not constructive. The generally expressed desire of "America first" cannot be criticized. It is a perfectly correct aspiration for our people to cherish. But the problem which we have to solve is how to make America first. It cannot be done by the cultivation of national bigotry, arrogance, or selfishness. Hatreds, jealousies, and suspicions will not be productive of any benefits in this direction. Here again we must apply the rule of toleration. Because there are other peoples whose ways are not our ways, and whose thoughts are not our thoughts, we are not warranted in drawing the conclusion that they are adding nothing to the sum of civilization. We can make little contribution to the welfare of humanity on the theory that we are a superior people and all others are an inferior people. We do not need to be too loud in the assertion of our own righteousness. It is true that we live under most favorable circumstances. But before we come to the final and irrevocable decision that we are better than everybody else, we need to consider what we might do if we had their provocations and their difficulties. We are not likely to improve our own condition or help humanity very much until we come to the sympathetic understanding that human nature is about the same everywhere, that it is rather evenly distributed over the surface of the earth, and that we are all united in a common brotherhood. We can only make America first in the true sense which that means by cultivating a spirit of friendship and good will, by the exercise of the virtues of patience and forbearance, by being "plenteous in mercy," and through progress at home and helpfulness abroad standing as an example of real service to humanity.

It is for these reasons that it seems clear that the results of the war will be lost and we shall only be entering a period of preparation for another conflict unless we can demobilize the racial antagonisms, fears, hatreds, and suspicions, and create an attitude of toleration in the public mind of the peoples of the earth. If our country is to have any position of leadership, I trust it may be in that direction, and I believe that the place where it should begin is at home. Let us cast off our hatreds. Let us candidly accept our treaties and our natural obligations of peace. We know and everyone knows that these old systems, antagonisms, and reliance on force have failed. If the world has made any progress, it has been the result of the development of other ideals. If we are to maintain and perfect our own civilization, if we are to be of any benefit to the rest of mankind, we must turn aside from the thoughts of destruction and cultivate the thoughts of construction. We cannot place our main reliance upon material forces. We must reaffirm and reinforce our ancient faith in truth and justice, in charitableness and tolerance. We must make our supreme commitment to the everlasting spiritual forces of life. We must mobilize the conscience of mankind.

Your gatherings are a living testimony of a determination to support these principles. It would be impossible to come into this presence, which is a symbol of more than three hundred years of our advancing civilization, which represents to such a degree the hope of our consecrated living and the prayers of our hallowed dead, without a firmer conviction of the deep and abiding purpose of our country to live in accordance with this vision. There have been and will be lapses and discouragements, surface storms and disturbances. The shallows will murmur, but the deep is still. We shall be made aware of the boisterous and turbulent forces of evil about us seeking the things which are temporal. But we shall also be made aware of the still small voice arising from the fireside of every devoted home in the land seeking the things which are eternal. To such a country, to such a cause, the American Legion has dedicated itself. Upon this rock you stand for the service of humanity. Against it no power can prevail.

THE INSPIRATION OF THE DECLARATION OF INDEPENDENCE
JULY 5, 1926

Calvin Coolidge is America's only president born on the Fourth of July. In 1926 he gave this address on the 150th anniversary of the Declaration of Independence. (He spoke on July 5 because July 4 fell

on a Sunday that year.) Coolidge used the occasion to emphasize that
all Americans held the rights identified in the Declaration. "If all
men are created equal, that is final," he said. "If they are endowed
with inalienable rights, that is final. If governments derive their just
power from the consent of the governed, that is final. No advance, no
progress can be made beyond these propositions." In response to pro-
gressives of his time (like those of ours) who suggested that America
had moved beyond the wisdom of the Founders, Coolidge called on
Americans not to "proclaim new theories and principles" but rather
to "reaffirm and reestablish those old theories and principles which
time and the unerring logic of events have demonstrated to be sound."

We meet to celebrate the birthday of America. The coming of
a new life always excites our interest. Although we know in
the case of the individual that it has been an infinite repetition
reaching back beyond our vision, that only makes it the more
wonderful. But how our interest and wonder increase when we
behold the miracle of the birth of a new nation. It is to pay
our tribute of reverence and respect to those who participated
in such a mighty event that we annually observe the fourth day
of July. Whatever may have been the impression created by the
news which went out from this city on that summer day in 1776,
there can be no doubt as to the estimate which is now placed
upon it. At the end of one hundred and fifty years, the four
corners of the earth unite in coming to Philadelphia as to a holy
shrine in grateful acknowledgment of a service so great, which a
few inspired men here rendered to humanity, that it is still the
preeminent support of free government throughout the world.

Although a century and a half measured in comparison
with the length of human experience is but a short time, yet
measured in the life of governments and nations it ranks as a
very respectable period. Certainly enough time has elapsed to

demonstrate with a great deal of thoroughness the value of our institutions and their dependability as rules for the regulation of human conduct and the advancement of civilization. They have been in existence long enough to become very well seasoned. They have met, and met successfully, the test of experience.

It is not so much then for the purpose of undertaking to proclaim new theories and principles that this annual celebration is maintained, but rather to reaffirm and reestablish those old theories and principles which time and the unerring logic of events have demonstrated to be sound. Amid all the clash of conflicting interests, amid all the welter of partisan politics, every American can turn for solace and consolation to the Declaration of Independence and the Constitution of the United States with the assurance and confidence that those two great charters of freedom and justice remain firm and unshaken. Whatever perils appear, whatever dangers threaten, the nation remains secure in the knowledge that the ultimate application of the law of the land will provide an adequate defense and protection.

It is little wonder that people at home and abroad consider Independence Hall as hallowed ground and revere the Liberty Bell as a sacred relic. That pile of bricks and mortar, that mass of metal, might appear to the uninstructed as only the outgrown meeting place and the shattered bell of a former time, useless now because of more modern conveniences, but to those who know they have become consecrated by the use which men have made of them. They have long been identified with a great cause. They are the framework of a spiritual event. The world looks upon them, because of their associations of one hundred and fifty years ago, as it looks upon the Holy Land because of what took place there nineteen hundred years ago. Through use for a righteous purpose they have become sanctified.

It is not here necessary to examine in detail the causes which led to the American Revolution. In their immediate occasion they were largely economic. The colonists objected to the navigation laws which interfered with their trade, they denied the power of Parliament to impose taxes which they were obliged to pay, and they therefore resisted the royal governors and the royal forces which were sent to secure obedience to these laws. But the conviction is inescapable that a new civilization had come, a new spirit had arisen on this side of the Atlantic more advanced and more developed in its regard for the rights of the individual than that which characterized the Old World. Life in a new and open country had aspirations which could not be realized in any subordinate position. A separate establishment was ultimately inevitable. It had been decreed by the very laws of human nature. Man everywhere has an unconquerable desire to be the master of his own destiny.

We are obliged to conclude that the Declaration of Independence represented the movement of a people. It was not, of course, a movement from the top. Revolutions do not come from that direction. It was not without the support of many of the most respectable people in the Colonies, who were entitled to all the consideration that is given to breeding, education, and possessions. It had the support of another element of great significance and importance to which I shall later refer. But the preponderance of all those who occupied a position which took on the aspect of aristocracy did not approve of the Revolution and held toward it an attitude either of neutrality or open hostility. It was in no sense a rising of the oppressed and downtrodden. It brought no scum to the surface, for the reason that colonial society had developed no scum. The great body of the people were accustomed to privations, but they were free from depravity. If they had poverty, it was not of the hopeless kind that afflicts great cities, but the inspiring kind that marks the spirit of the pioneer. The American Revolution represented the informed and mature convictions of a great mass of independent, liberty-loving, God-fearing people who knew their rights and possessed the courage to dare to maintain them. The Continental Congress was not only composed of great men but it represented a great people. While its members did not fail to exercise a remarkable leadership, they were equally observant of their representative capacity. They were industrious in encouraging their constituents to instruct them to support independence. But until such instructions were given, they were inclined to withhold action.

While North Carolina has the honor of first authorizing its delegates to concur with other Colonies in declaring independence, it was quickly followed by South Carolina and Georgia, which also gave general instructions broad enough to include such action. But the first instructions which unconditionally directed its delegates to declare for independence came from the great Commonwealth of Virginia. These were immediately followed by Rhode Island and Massachusetts, while the other Colonies, with the exception of New York, soon adopted a like course.

This obedience of the delegates to the wishes of their constituents, which in some cases caused them to modify their previous positions, is a matter of great significance. It reveals an orderly process of government in the first place; but more than that, it demonstrates that the Declaration of Independence was the result of the seasoned and deliberate thought of the dominant portion of the people of the Colonies. Adopted after long discussion and as the result of the duly authorized expression of the preponderance of public opinion, it did not partake of dark intrigue or hidden conspiracy. It was well advised. It had

about it nothing of the lawless and disordered nature of a riot-
ous insurrection. It was maintained on a plane which rises above
the ordinary conception of rebellion. It was in no sense a radical movement but took on the dignity of a resistance to illegal
usurpations. It was conservative and represented the action of
the colonists to maintain their constitutional rights, which from
time immemorial had been guaranteed to them under the law
of the land.

When we come to examine the action of the Continental
Congress in adopting the Declaration of Independence in the
light of what was set out in that great document and in the light
of succeeding events, we cannot escape the conclusion that it
had a much broader and deeper significance than a mere seces-
sion of territory and the establishment of a new nation. Events
of that nature have been taking place since the dawn of history.
One empire after another has arisen, only to crumble away as its
constituent parts separated from each other and set up independent governments of their own. Such actions long ago became
commonplace. They have occurred too often to hold the attention of the world and command the admiration and reverence
of humanity. There is something beyond the establishment of a
new nation, great as that event would be, in the Declaration of
Independence which has ever since caused it to be regarded as
one of the great charters that not only was to liberate America
but was everywhere to ennoble humanity.

It was not because it was proposed to establish a new nation,
but because it was proposed to establish a nation on new principles, that July 4, 1776, has come to be regarded as one of the
greatest days in history. Great ideas do not burst upon the world
unannounced. They are reached by a gradual development over
a length of time usually proportionate to their importance. This
is especially true of the principles laid down in the Declaration

of Independence. Three very definite propositions were set out in its preamble regarding the nature of mankind and therefore of government. These were the doctrine that all men are created equal, that they are endowed with certain inalienable rights, and that therefore the source of the just powers of government must be derived from the consent of the governed.

If no one is to be accounted as born into a superior station, if there is to be no ruling class, and if all possess rights which can neither be bartered away nor taken from them by any earthly power, it follows as a matter of course that the practical authority of the Government has to rest on the consent of the governed. While these principles were not altogether new in political action, and were very far from new in political speculation, they had never been assembled before and declared in such a combination. But remarkable as this may be, it is not the chief distinction of the Declaration of Independence. The importance of political speculation is not to be underestimated, as I shall presently disclose. Until the idea is developed and the plan made, there can be no action.

It was the fact that our Declaration of Independence containing these immortal truths was the political action of a duly authorized and constituted representative public body in its sovereign capacity, supported by the force of general opinion and by the armies of Washington already in the field, which makes it the most important civil document in the world. It was not only the principles declared, but the fact that therewith a new nation was born which was to be founded upon those principles and which from that time forth in its development has actually maintained those principles, that makes this pronouncement an incomparable event in the history of government. It was an assertion that a people had arisen determined to make every necessary sacrifice for the support of these truths and by their practical application bring the War of Independence to a successful conclusion and adopt the Constitution of the United States with all that it has meant to civilization.

The idea that the people have a right to choose their own rulers was not new in political history. It was the foundation of every popular attempt to depose an undesirable king. This right was set out with a good deal of detail by the Dutch when as early as July 26, 1581, they declared their independence of Philip of Spain. In their long struggle with the Stuarts, the British people asserted the same principles, which finally culminated in the Bill of Rights deposing the last of that house and placing William and Mary on the throne. In each of these cases, sovereignty through divine right was displaced by sovereignty through the consent of the people. Running through the same documents, though expressed in different terms, is the clear inference of inalienable rights. But we should search these charters in vain for an assertion of the doctrine of equality. This principle had not before appeared as an official political declaration of any nation. It was profoundly revolutionary. It is one of the corner stones of American institutions.

But if these truths to which the declaration refers have not before been adopted in their combined entirety by national authority, it is a fact that they had been long pondered and often expressed in political speculation. It is generally assumed that French thought had some effect upon our public mind during Revolutionary days. This may have been true. But the principles of our declaration had been under discussion in the Colonies for nearly two generations before the advent of the French political philosophy that characterized the middle of the eighteenth century. In fact, they come from an earlier date. A very positive echo of what the Dutch had done in 1581, and what the English were preparing to do, appears in the assertion of the Rev. Thomas Hooker of Connecticut as early as 1638, when he said in a sermon before the General Court that:

The foundation of authority is laid in the free consent of the people.

The choice of public magistrates belongs unto the people by God's own allowance.

This doctrine found wide acceptance among the nonconformist clergy who later made up the Congregational Church. The great apostle of this movement was the Rev. John Wise, of Massachusetts. He was one of the leaders of the revolt against the royal governor Andros in 1687, for which he suffered imprisonment. He was a liberal in ecclesiastical controversies. He appears to have been familiar with the writings of the political scientist Samuel Pufendorf, who was born in Saxony in 1632. Wise published a treatise, entitled "The Church's Quarrel Espoused," in 1710 which was amplified in another publication in 1717. In it he dealt with the principles of civil government. His works were reprinted in 1772 and have been declared to have been nothing less than a textbook of liberty for our Revolutionary fathers.

While the written word was the foundation, it is apparent that the spoken word was the vehicle for convincing the people. This came with great force and wide range from the successors of Hooker and Wise. It was carried on with a missionary spirit which did not fail to reach the Scotch Irish of North Carolina, showing its influence by significantly making that Colony the first to give instructions to its delegates looking to independence. This preaching reached the neighborhood of Thomas Jefferson, who acknowledged that his "best ideas of democracy" had been secured at church meetings.

That these ideas were prevalent in Virginia is further revealed by the Declaration of Rights, which was prepared by George Mason and presented to the general assembly on May 27, 1776. This document asserted popular sovereignty and inherent natural rights, but confined the doctrine of equality to the assertion that "All men are created equally free and independent." It can scarcely be imagined that Jefferson was unacquainted with what had been done in his own Commonwealth of Virginia when he took up the task of drafting the Declaration of Independence. But these thoughts can very largely be traced back to what John Wise was writing in 1710. He said, "Every man must be acknowledged equal to every man." Again, "The end of all good government is to cultivate humanity and promote the happiness of all and the good of every man in all his rights, his life, liberty, estate, honor, and so forth...." And again, "For as they have a power every man in his natural state, so upon combination they can and do bequeath this power to others and settle it according as their united discretion shall determine." And still again, "Democracy is Christ's government in church and state." Here was the doctrine of equality, popular sovereignty, and the substance of the theory of inalienable rights clearly asserted by Wise at the opening of the eighteenth century, just as we have the principle of the consent of the governed stated by Hooker as early as 1638.

When we take all these circumstances into consideration, it is but natural that the first paragraph of the Declaration of Independence should open with a reference to Nature's God and should close in the final paragraphs with an appeal to the Supreme Judge of the world and an assertion of a firm reliance on Divine Providence. Coming from these sources, having as it did this background, it is no wonder that Samuel Adams could say "The people seem to recognize this resolution as though it were a decree promulgated from heaven."

No one can examine this record and escape the conclusion that in the great outline of its principles, the Declaration was the result of the religious teachings of the preceding period. The profound philosophy which Jonathan Edwards applied to theology, the popular preaching of George Whitefield, had aroused the thought and stirred the people of the Colonies in preparation for this great event. No doubt the speculations which had been going on in England, and especially on the Continent, lent their influence to the general sentiment of the times. Of course, the world is always influenced by all the experience and all the thought of the past. But when we come to a contemplation of the immediate conception of the principles of human relationship which went into the Declaration of Independence, we are not required to extend our search beyond our own shores. They are found in the texts, the sermons, and the writings of the early colonial clergy who were earnestly undertaking to instruct their congregations in the great mystery of how to live. They preached equality because they believed in the fatherhood of God and the brotherhood of man. They justified freedom by the text that we are all created in the divine image, all partakers of the divine spirit.

Placing every man on a plane where he acknowledged no superiors, where no one possessed any right to rule over him, he must inevitably choose his own rulers through a system of self-government. This was their theory of democracy. In those days such doctrines would scarcely have been permitted to flourish and spread in any other country. This was the purpose which the fathers cherished. In order that they might have freedom to express these thoughts and opportunity to put them into action, whole congregations with their pastors had migrated to the colonies. These great truths were in the air that our people breathed. Whatever else we may say of it, the Declaration of Independence was profoundly American.

If this apprehension of the facts be correct, and the documentary evidence would appear to verify it, then certain conclusions are bound to follow. A spring will cease to flow if its source be dried up; a tree will wither if its roots be destroyed. In its main features the Declaration of Independence is a great spiritual document. It is a declaration not of material but of spiritual conceptions. Equality, liberty, popular sovereignty, the rights of man—these are not elements which we can see and touch. They are ideals. They have their source and their roots in the religious convictions. They belong to the unseen world. Unless the faith of the American people in these religious convictions is to endure, the principles of our Declaration will perish. We cannot continue to enjoy the result if we neglect and abandon the cause.

We are too prone to overlook another conclusion. Governments do not make ideals, but ideals make governments. This is both historically and logically true. Of course the government can help to sustain ideals and can create institutions through which they can be the better observed, but their source by their very nature is in the people. The people have to bear their own responsibilities. There is no method by which that burden can be shifted to the government. It is not the enactment but the observance of laws that creates the character of a nation.

About the Declaration there is a finality that is exceedingly restful. It is often asserted that the world has made a great deal of progress since 1776, that we have had new thoughts and new experiences which have given us a great advance over the people of that day, and that we may therefore very well discard their conclusions for something more modern. But that reasoning cannot be applied to this great charter. If all men are created equal, that is final. If they are endowed with inalienable rights, that is final. If governments derive their just powers from the consent of the governed, that is final. No advance, no progress can be made beyond these propositions. If anyone wishes to deny their truth or their soundness, the only direction in which he can proceed historically is not forward but backward toward the time when there was no equality, no rights of the individual, no rule of the people. Those who wish to proceed in that direction cannot lay claim to progress. They are reactionary. Their ideas are not more modern but more ancient than those of the Revolutionary fathers.

In the development of its institutions, America can fairly claim that it has remained true to the principles which were declared 150 years ago. In all the essentials, we have achieved an equality which was never possessed by any other people. Even in the less important matter of material possessions, we have secured a wider and wider distribution of wealth. The rights of the individual are held sacred and protected by constitutional guarantees, which even the government itself is bound not to violate. If there is any one thing among us that is established beyond question, it is self-government; the right of the people to rule. If there is any failure in respect to any of these principles, it is because there is a failure on the part of individuals to observe them. We hold that the duly authorized expression of the will of the people has a divine sanction. But even in that we come back to the theory of John Wise that "Democracy is Christ's government." The ultimate sanction of law rests on the righteous authority of the Almighty.

On an occasion like this, a great temptation exists to present evidence of the practical success of our form of democratic republic at home and the ever broadening acceptance it is securing abroad. Although these things are well known, their frequent consideration is an encouragement and an inspiration. But it is not results and effects so much as sources and causes that

I believe it is even more necessary constantly to contemplate. Ours is a government of the people. It represents their will. Its officers may sometimes go astray, but that is not a reason for criticizing the principles of our institutions. The real heart of the American government depends upon the heart of the people. It is from that source that we must look for all genuine reform. It is to that cause that we must ascribe all our results.

It was in the contemplation of these truths that the fathers made their declaration and adopted their Constitution. It was to establish a free government, which must not be permitted to degenerate into the unrestrained authority of a mere majority or the unbridled weight of a mere influential few. They undertook to balance these interests against each other and provide the three separate independent branches—the executive, the legislative, and the judicial departments of the government— with checks against each other in order that neither one might encroach upon the other. These are our guarantees of liberty. As a result of these methods, enterprise has been duly protected from confiscation, the people have been free from oppression, and there has been an ever broadening and deepening of the humanities of life.

Under a system of popular government, there will always be those who will seek for political preferment by clamoring for reform. While there is very little of this which is not sincere, there is a large portion that is not well informed. In my opinion, very little of just criticism can attach to the theories and principles of our institutions. There is far more danger of harm than there is hope of good in any radical changes. We do need a better understanding and comprehension of them and a better knowledge of the foundations of government in general. Our forefathers came to certain conclusions and decided upon certain courses of action which have been a great blessing to the world.

Before we can understand their conclusions, we must go back and review the course which they followed. We must think the thoughts which they thought. Their intellectual life centered around the meetinghouse. They were intent upon religious worship. While there were always among them men of deep learning, and later those who had comparatively large possessions, the mind of the people was not so much engrossed in how much they knew or how much they had as in how they were going to live. While scantily provided with other literature, there was a wide acquaintance with the Scriptures. Over a period as great as that which measures the existence of our independence, they were subject to this discipline not only in their religious life and educational training but also in their political thought. They were a people who came under the influence of a great spiritual development and acquired a great moral power.

No other theory is adequate to explain or comprehend the Declaration of Independence. It is the product of the spiritual insight of the people. We live in an age of science and of abounding accumulation of material things. These did not create our Declaration. Our Declaration created them. The things of the spirit come first. Unless we cling to that, all our material prosperity, overwhelming though it may appear, will turn to a barren scepter in our grasp. If we are to maintain the great heritage which has been bequeathed to us, we must be like-minded as the fathers who created it. We must not sink into a pagan materialism. We must cultivate the reverence which they had for the things that are holy. We must follow the spiritual and moral leadership which they showed. We must keep replenished, that they may glow with a more compelling flame, the altar fires before which they worshipped.

ACKNOWLEDGMENTS

The Calvin Coolidge Presidential Foundation is grateful to the Coolidge family for its enthusiastic support of this new edition of *The Autobiography of Calvin Coolidge*. Jennifer Coolidge Harville, John Whitman Sayles, and Christopher Coolidge Jeter—President and Mrs. Coolidge's great-grandchildren—graciously extended copyright permission for this edition.

Special thanks goes to the Intercollegiate Studies Institute and Jed Donahue for their patience and skill in preparing this publication. Jed showed enthusiasm from the beginning, and his knowledge of Coolidge greatly enhanced this edition. Managing editor Anthony Sacramone expertly shepherded the book to press.

The work of a number of researchers and contributors made this publication possible. C. C. Borzilleri devoted many hours to locating photos and helping prepare the manuscript. William Pettinger provided research support. Clark Donovan provided strong assistance in preparing footnotes. John Ferrell deserves thanks for his assistance maintaining the Coolidge Foundation's archives in Vermont, which proved indispensable to this project. Rob Hammer and Jared Rhoads cheered the project along. Previous Coolidge Foundation archivists,

Kate Bradley especially, are to be commended for their careful preservation of the Foundation's collection over the years.

The Coolidge Foundation also thanks a number of individuals and institutions for their archival and photographic research. William Jenney, Tracy Martin, and Laura Trieschmann of the Vermont Division for Historic Preservation supplied useful photographs and advice. Julie Bartlett Nelson and the Forbes Library also provided valuable archival and photographic research for this book. Bob Cullum and the rest of Leslie Jones's family furnished a number of wonderful images of Coolidge's life from the Boston Public Library's Leslie Jones Collection. Chris Barber of the Archives Division at Amherst College provided an image from Coolidge's time studying there. Paul Carnahan and the Vermont Historical Society also assisted with archival and photographic research, and kindly extended photo permissions. Additionally, Getty, Alamy, and the Library of Congress all contributed images to this volume.

Furthermore, the Coolidge Foundation is thankful for the support and assistance of its board of trustees as well as its friends and supporters from across America. Milt and Debbie Valera of the National Notary Foundation have been critical to keeping the *Autobiography* in print over the years. So have James Ottaway Jr., Robert Kirby, Cyndy Bittinger, Mimi Baird, and Jim Cooke. The fine research of academics who came before us, including the late Edward Connery Lathem, Hendrik Booraem, Robert Sobel, and Robert Ferrell, helped us to construct the footnotes. The writings of Craig Fehrman and Jerry Wallace also proved valuable. Governor James H. Douglas, vice chair of the Coolidge Foundation, improved the product and penned a superb essay to accompany this edition.

Finally, the Coolidge Foundation owes its greatest debt to Calvin Coolidge for "bending his energies," as he would put it, in service of our republic.

Amity Shlaes and Matthew Denhart
Calvin Coolidge Presidential Foundation, 2020

INDEX

234

ABOUT THE COOLIDGE FOUNDATION

The Calvin Coolidge Presidential Foundation is the official foundation dedicated to preserving the legacy and advancing the values of America's thirtieth president. In the absence of an official, federally funded presidential library, the Coolidge Foundation was formed in 1960 by John Coolidge, the president's son, along with a group of fellow Coolidge enthusiasts. The Foundation is based at the president's birthplace in Plymouth Notch, Vermont. There it joins its longtime partner, the state of Vermont, in hosting visitors throughout the summer season. At Coolidge House in Washington, D.C., the Foundation maintains another Coolidge exhibit. Wherever it operates, the Foundation seeks to increase Americans' understanding of President Coolidge and the values he championed.

The Foundation's signature initiative is the Coolidge Scholars Program, a full-ride, four-year, merit scholarship that recipients can use at any accredited college or university in the United States. Each year thousands of high school students study President Coolidge and read his autobiography through the course of applying for the scholarship. Currently, three to four new Coolidge Scholars are selected annually, and a group of one hundred top applicants earn the distinction of "Coolidge Senator." The Foundation also operates a national high school debate program, the Coolidge Cup. From across the nation, debaters converge to compete for the Coolidge Cup on the Fourth of July, Coolidge's birthday, in Plymouth Notch. To date, more than 2,000 students have participated in Coolidge League debate.

We invite you to join our work in sharing Silent Cal with the nation. For more information about how to get involved, please visit us online at **CoolidgeFoundation.org**.